California Post
Exam Study Guide

California Police Officer Exam Prep Team

Table of Contents

Quick Overview

As you draw closer to taking your exam, effective preparation becomes more and more important. Thankfully, you have this study guide to help you get ready. Use this guide to help keep your studying on track and refer to it often.

This study guide contains several key sections that will help you be successful on your exam. The guide contains tips for what you should do the night before and the day of the test. Also included are test-taking tips. Knowing the right information is not always enough. Many well-prepared test takers struggle with exams. These tips will help equip you to accurately read, assess, and answer test questions.

A large part of the guide is devoted to showing you what content to expect on the exam and to helping you better understand that content. Near the end of this guide is a practice test so that you can see how well you have grasped the content. Then, answer explanations are provided so that you can understand why you missed certain questions.

Don't try to cram the night before you take your exam. This is not a wise strategy for a few reasons. First, your retention of the information will be low. Your time would be better used by reviewing information you already know rather than trying to learn a lot of new information. Second, you will likely become stressed as you try to gain a large amount of knowledge in a short amount of time. Third, you will be depriving yourself of sleep. So be sure to go to bed at a reasonable time the night before. Being well-rested helps you focus and remain calm.

Be sure to eat a substantial breakfast the morning of the exam. If you are taking the exam in the afternoon, be sure to have a good lunch as well. Being hungry is distracting and can make it difficult to focus. You have hopefully spent lots of time preparing for the exam. Don't let an empty stomach get in the way of success!

When travelling to the testing center, leave earlier than needed. That way, you have a buffer in case you experience any delays. This will help you remain calm and will keep you from missing your appointment time at the testing center.

Be sure to pace yourself during the exam. Don't try to rush through the exam. There is no need to risk performing poorly on the exam just so you can leave the testing center early. Allow yourself to use all of the allotted time if needed.

Remain positive while taking the exam even if you feel like you are performing poorly. Thinking about the content you should have mastered will not help you perform better on the exam.

Once the exam is complete, take some time to relax. Even if you feel that you need to take the exam again, you will be well served by some down time before you begin studying again. It's often easier to convince yourself to study if you know that it will come with a reward!

Test-Taking Strategies

1. Predicting the Answer

When you feel confident in your preparation for a multiple-choice test, try predicting the answer before reading the answer choices. This is especially useful on questions that test objective factual knowledge or that ask you to fill in a blank. By predicting the answer before reading the available choices, you eliminate the possibility that you will be distracted or led astray by an incorrect answer choice. You will feel more confident in your selection if you read the question, predict the answer, and then find your prediction among the answer choices. After using this strategy, be sure to still read all of the answer choices carefully and completely. If you feel unprepared, you should not attempt to predict the answers. This would be a waste of time and an opportunity for your mind to wander in the wrong direction.

2. Reading the Whole Question

Too often, test takers scan a multiple-choice question, recognize a few familiar words, and immediately jump to the answer choices. Test authors are aware of this common impatience, and they will sometimes prey upon it. For instance, a test author might subtly turn the question into a negative, or he or she might redirect the focus of the question right at the end. The only way to avoid falling into these traps is to read the entirety of the question carefully before reading the answer choices.

3. Looking for Wrong Answers

Long and complicated multiple-choice questions can be intimidating. One way to simplify a difficult multiple-choice question is to eliminate all of the answer choices that are clearly wrong. In most sets of answers, there will be at least one selection that can be dismissed right away. If the test is administered on paper, the test taker could draw a line through it to indicate that it may be ignored; otherwise, the test taker will have to perform this operation mentally or on scratch paper. In either case, once the obviously incorrect answers have been eliminated, the remaining choices may be considered. Sometimes identifying the clearly wrong answers will give the test taker some information about the correct answer. For instance, if one of the remaining answer choices is a direct opposite of one of the eliminated answer choices, it may well be the correct answer. The opposite of obviously wrong is obviously right! Of course, this is not always the case. Some answers are obviously incorrect simply because they are irrelevant to the question being asked. Still, identifying and eliminating some incorrect answer choices is a good way to simplify a multiple-choice question.

4. Don't Overanalyze

Anxious test takers often overanalyze questions. When you are nervous, your brain will often run wild, causing you to make associations and discover clues that don't actually exist. If you feel that this may be a problem for you, do whatever you can to slow down during the test. Try taking a deep breath or counting to ten. As you read and consider the question, restrict yourself to the particular words used by the author. Avoid thought tangents about what the author *really* meant, or what he or she was *trying* to say. The only things that matter on a multiple-choice test are the words that are actually in the question. You must avoid reading too much into a multiple-choice question, or supposing that the writer meant something other than what he or she wrote.

5. No Need for Panic

It is wise to learn as many strategies as possible before taking a multiple-choice test, but it is likely that you will come across a few questions for which you simply don't know the answer. In this situation, avoid panicking. Because most multiple-choice tests include dozens of questions, the relative value of a single wrong answer is small. Moreover, your failure on one question has no effect on your success elsewhere on the test. As much as possible, you should compartmentalize each question on a multiple-choice test. In other words, you should not allow your feelings about one question to affect your success on the others. When you find a question that you either don't understand or don't know how to answer, just take a deep breath and do your best. Read the entire question slowly and carefully. Try rephrasing the question a couple of different ways. Then, read all of the answer choices carefully. After eliminating obviously wrong answers, make a selection and move on to the next question.

6. Confusing Answer Choices

When working on a difficult multiple-choice question, there may be a tendency to focus on the answer choices that are the easiest to understand. Many people, whether consciously or not, gravitate to the answer choices that require the least concentration, knowledge, and memory. This is a mistake. When you come across an answer choice that is confusing, you should give it extra attention. A question might be confusing because you do not know the subject matter to which it refers. If this is the case, don't eliminate the answer before you have affirmatively settled on another. When you come across an answer choice of this type, set it aside as you look at the remaining choices. If you can confidently assert that one of the other choices is correct, you can leave the confusing answer aside. Otherwise, you will need to take a moment to try to better understand the confusing answer choice. Rephrasing is one way to tease out the sense of a confusing answer choice.

7. Your First Instinct

Many people struggle with multiple-choice tests because they overthink the questions. If you have studied sufficiently for the test, you should be prepared to trust your first instinct once you have carefully and completely read the question and all of the answer choices. There is a great deal of research suggesting that the mind can come to the correct conclusion very quickly once it has obtained all of the relevant information. At times, it may seem to you as if your intuition is working faster even than your reasoning mind. This may in fact be true. The knowledge you obtain while studying may be retrieved from your subconscious before you have a chance to work out the associations that support it. Verify your instinct by working out the reasons that it should be trusted.

8. Key Words

Many test takers struggle with multiple-choice questions because they have poor reading comprehension skills. Quickly reading and understanding a multiple-choice question requires a mixture of skill and experience. To help with this, try jotting down a few key words and phrases on a piece of scrap paper. Doing this concentrates the process of reading and forces the mind to weigh the relative importance of the question's parts. In selecting words and phrases to write down, the test taker thinks about the question more deeply and carefully. This is especially true for multiple-choice questions that are preceded by a long prompt.

9. Subtle Negatives

One of the oldest tricks in the multiple-choice test writer's book is to subtly reverse the meaning of a question with a word like *not* or *except*. If you are not paying attention to each word in the question, you can easily be led astray by this trick. For instance, a common question format is, "Which of the following is…?" Obviously, if the question instead is, "Which of the following is not…?," then the answer will be quite different. Even worse, the test makers are aware of the potential for this mistake and will include one answer choice that would be correct if the question were not negated or reversed. A test taker who misses the reversal will find what he or she believes to be a correct answer and will be so confident that he or she will fail to reread the question and discover the original error. The only way to avoid this is to practice a wide variety of multiple-choice questions and to pay close attention to each and every word.

10. Reading Every Answer Choice

It may seem obvious, but you should always read every one of the answer choices! Too many test takers fall into the habit of scanning the question and assuming that they understand the question because they recognize a few key words. From there, they pick the first answer choice that answers the question they believe they have read. Test takers who read all of the answer choices might discover that one of the latter answer choices is actually *more* correct. Moreover, reading all of the answer choices can remind you of facts related to the question that can help you arrive at the correct answer. Sometimes, a misstatement or incorrect detail in one of the latter answer choices will trigger your memory of the subject and will enable you to find the right answer. Failing to read all of the answer choices is like not reading all of the items on a restaurant menu: you might miss out on the perfect choice.

11. Spot the Hedges

One of the keys to success on multiple-choice tests is paying close attention to every word. This is never more true than with words like *almost*, *most*, *some*, and *sometimes*. These words are called "hedges" because they indicate that a statement is not totally true or not true in every place and time. An absolute statement will contain no hedges, but in many subjects, like literature and history, the answers are not always straightforward or absolute. There are always exceptions to the rules in these subjects. For this reason, you should favor those multiple-choice questions that contain hedging language. The presence of qualifying words indicates that the author is taking special care with his or her words, which is certainly important when composing the right answer. After all, there are many ways to be wrong, but there is only one way to be right! For this reason, it is wise to avoid answers that are absolute when taking a multiple-choice test. An absolute answer is one that says things are either all one way or all another. They often include words like *every*, *always*, *best*, and *never*. If you are taking a multiple-choice test in a subject that doesn't lend itself to absolute answers, be on your guard if you see any of these words.

12. Long Answers

In many subject areas, the answers are not simple. As already mentioned, the right answer often requires hedges. Another common feature of the answers to a complex or subjective question are qualifying clauses, which are groups of words that subtly modify the meaning of the sentence. If the question or answer choice describes a rule to which there are exceptions or the subject matter is complicated, ambiguous, or confusing, the correct answer will require many words in order to be expressed clearly and accurately. In essence, you should not be deterred by answer choices that seem excessively long. Oftentimes, the author of the text will not be able to write the correct answer without offering some qualifications and modifications. Your job is to read the answer choices thoroughly and completely and to select the one that most accurately and precisely answers the question.

13. Restating to Understand

Sometimes, a question on a multiple-choice test is difficult not because of what it asks but because of how it is written. If this is the case, restate the question or answer choice in different words. This process serves a couple of important purposes. First, it forces you to concentrate on the core of the question. In order to rephrase the question accurately, you have to understand it well. Rephrasing the question will concentrate your mind on the key words and ideas. Second, it will present the information to your mind in a fresh way. This process may trigger your memory and render some useful scrap of information picked up while studying.

14. True Statements

Sometimes an answer choice will be true in itself, but it does not answer the question. This is one of the main reasons why it is essential to read the question carefully and completely before proceeding to the answer choices. Too often, test takers skip ahead to the answer choices and look for true statements. Having found one of these, they are content to select it without reference to the question above. Obviously, this provides an easy way for test makers to play tricks. The savvy test taker will always read the entire question before turning to the answer choices. Then, having settled on a correct answer choice, he or she will refer to the original question and ensure that the selected answer is relevant. The mistake of choosing a correct-but-irrelevant answer choice is especially common on questions related to specific pieces of objective knowledge, like historical or scientific facts. A prepared test taker will have a wealth of factual knowledge at his or her disposal, and should not be careless in its application.

15. No Patterns

One of the more dangerous ideas that circulates about multiple-choice tests is that the correct answers tend to fall into patterns. These erroneous ideas range from a belief that B and C are the most common right answers, to the idea that an unprepared test-taker should answer "A-B-A-C-A-D-A-B-A." It cannot be emphasized enough that pattern-seeking of this type is exactly the WRONG way to approach a multiple-choice test. To begin with, it is highly unlikely that the test maker will plot the correct answers according to some predetermined pattern. The questions are scrambled and delivered in a random order. Furthermore, even if the test maker was following a pattern in the assignation of correct answers, there is no reason why the test taker would know which pattern he or she was using. Any attempt to discern a pattern in the answer choices is a waste of time and a distraction from the real work of taking the test. A test taker would be much better served by extra preparation before the test than by reliance on a pattern in the answers.

California Post Introduction

Function of the Test

California POST (Peace Officer Standards and Training) administers the POST Entry-Level Law Enforcement Test Battery (PELLETB) to prospective officers for various law enforcement agencies California. California law requires that law enforcement officers be able to read and write at a level sufficient to perform the job of a peace officer. This is determined by the use of the PELLETB or other professionally developed and validated test of reading and writing ability. Accordingly, the PELLETB tests language aptitude, with sections covering both writing ability and reading ability. PELLETB scores are used by California law enforcement agencies as an indicator of a candidate's readiness for a career in law enforcement. The PELLETB is typically administered before a prospective officer is admitted to a police academy, and can be used by agencies as part of their hiring decisions.

Test Administration

The test is usually given free to all California law enforcement applicants. Applicants may be directed to take the test by the law enforcement agency to which they are applying, or they may contact an agency directly and register to take the test through that agency. The test is offered frequently, but not at any set state-wide time or date. Instead, local agencies determine when and where to administer the test.

Test-takers can retake the test, but must wait at least one month after taking the test to take it again. Test-takers with disabilities may seek appropriate accommodations through the agency offering the PELLETB.

Test Format

The test must be completed within two hours and thirty minutes. The test is administered in a written format, and is comprised of 105 multiple-choice, fill-in-the-blank questions covering reading, writing, and reasoning.

Component	Sub-Test	Questions	Description
Reading	Comprehension	20	Answer questions about a passage
Reading	CLOZE	40	Fill in a passage's missing words from context
Reasoning	Reasoning	16	Analyze patterns to answer questions
Writing	Clarity	15	ID which sentence is clearest
Writing	Spelling	15	Fill blank with properly spelled word
Writing	Vocabulary	15	ID the best synonym

The reading section is broken down into two sub-tests, comprehension and the CLOZE. The reading comprehension section asks test-takers to read a brief passage and answer multiple choice questions about the meaning of the passage. The CLOZE, often considered the most difficult sub-test, involves a passage in which specific words have been removed. Test-takers must determine from context what word appropriately fills the blanks thereby created.

The writing section is comprised of three sub-tests, clarity, spelling, and vocabulary. In the clarity sub-test, test-takers must determine which of two sentences is written more clearly. In the spelling sub-test, they must pick the correctly spelled word from four choices. In the vocabulary sub-test, they must identify the best synonym for a given word from four choices.

Finally, the reasoning sub-test presents the test-taker with patterns of letters, numbers, or shapes. The test-taker must analyze the patterns and answer questions about them.

Scoring

Prospective law enforcement officers who complete the PELLETB will receive a score known as a "T-score." A T-score is a standardized score that fits the performance of test-takers to a normalized curve. The average test-taker will receive a T-score of 50, and each standard deviation above or below the average will get a score 10 points higher or lower than 50. There is no set passing score, as different agencies will use different criteria at different times. However, a typical agency might set a minimum score between 40 and 45 for admission to their academy. Scores are generally returned to the agency (not the applicant) within about two weeks, and the agencies are required to provide applicants with their results within 30 days.

Clarity

In today's law enforcement world, the ability to write clearly and effectively is an important skill. Written communications such as incident reports and arrest reports are an integral part of the job, and being able to produce clear, comprehensive communications is essential.

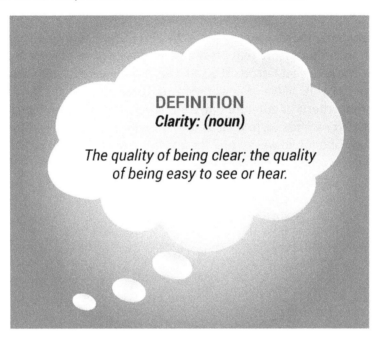

Clear written communication is important in everyday life—particularly in law enforcement. Officers are often responsible for creating a variety of daily reports, and writing content that's clear and concise results in more effective communications.

This section of the study guide focuses on writing *clarity*. The definition of clarity is "the quality of being clear." In writing, this means that the content is focused and the writer's intention is clear in both word choice and sentence structure. Simply put, the writing is clear. Why is this important? Writers want their readers to understand exactly what they're saying and NOT misinterpret their words. In the same sense, readers want a clear understanding of what they're reading. The following section covers understanding writing clarity through basic grammar principles.

Subjects and Predicates

Subjects
Every complete sentence is made up of two parts: a subject and a predicate. The *subject* is *who* or *what* the sentence is about. There are three subject types: simple, complete, and compound.

A *simple subject* tells *who* or *what* the sentence is about without additional details. For example:

> The blue car won the race.

In this sentence, the simple subject is the word *car*.

A *complete subject* contains the simple subject and its modifiers. In writing, a *modifier* is a word or phrase that gives more detail about a part of the sentence. In this case, the modifier gives more information about the subject. When looking for a complete subject, first identify the verb or action word in the sentence (e.g., *run, jump, carried*), then ask to *who* or *what* the verb is referring. Look again at the previous example:

> Sentence: The blue car won the race.
>
> Identify the verb: *won*
>
> Ask who or what won: *The blue car*
>
> Answer: *The blue car* is the complete subject because it answers *what* won. Notice how the complete subject includes the simple subject (*car*) along with its modifier (*blue*).

If there's more than one subject in a sentence, it's called a *compound subject*. Look at the sentence below and identify the compound subject:

> Sentence: John and I jumped over the huge puddle in the parking lot.
>
> Identify the verb: *jumped*
>
> Ask who or what jumped: *John and I*
>
> Answer: *John and I* is the compound subject of the sentence because more than one subject can answer the question of *who* jumped over the puddle.

Predicates

In a sentence, the *predicate* usually tells something about the subject by describing what the subject does, is, or has. Similar to subjects, predicates are simple, complete, or compound.

A *simple predicate* is simply the verb. For example:

> The dog ran into the busy road.

In this sentence, the simple predicate is the word *ran*.

A *complete predicate* contains the verb as well as its modifiers. In the example above, the complete predicate is *ran into the busy road*.

A *compound predicate* is when two or more words describe one subject. For example:

> The flight was delayed and eventually canceled.

In this sentence, the compound predicate (*was delayed and eventually canceled*) provides two details about one subject (*The flight*).

<u>Modeling Subjects and Predicates in a Sentence Diagram</u>

A *sentence diagram* makes it easier to identify the subject and predicate in a sentence. To create one, draw a long horizontal line with a short vertical line going through it. Write the subject of the sentence to the left of the vertical line and the predicate to the right. Here's an example:

<u>The black pen | ran out of ink on the last page of the document.</u>

(*SUBJECT*)   (*PREDICATE*)

The vertical line divides the subject (*The black pen*) from the predicate (*ran out of ink*).

Subject-Verb Agreement

The basic rule of subject-verb agreement is that a *singular subject* (one person, place, or thing) requires a singular verb, while a *plural subject* (more than one person, place, or thing) needs a plural verb.

When a sentence is in the present tense and contains a singular subject, the singular verb usually ends with the letter *s*. For example:

Riley stacks the books on the shelf.

Since the subject (*Riley*) is singular, the verb needs to be singular (*stacks*). If the subject is plural, the verb must also be plural:

Riley and Nate stack the books on the shelf.

In this sentence the subject is plural (*Riley and Nate*) so the verb must be plural (*stack*). Subjects can be nouns (as above) or pronouns. When the subject is a singular pronoun such as *I* or *you*, the verb is also singular. In the case of *I* or *you*, though the verb is singular, it usually will not have an *s* on the end. For example:

Can *you call* for the pizza in ten minutes?

In this case the subject (*you*) is singular, so the verb (*call*) is also singular.

Subjects and verbs must also agree in point of view (POV) and verb tense (past, present, or future). The first-, second-, and third-person point-of-view pronouns (singular and plural) are shown below:

	First-Person POV	Second-Person POV	Third-Person POV
Singular Pronoun	*I*	*You*	*He/She/It*
Plural Pronoun	*We*	*You*	*They*

Using the chart above, look at the following examples of subject-verb agreement in relation to point of view and verb tense (in this case, present tense):

	Singular Verb	Plural Verb
First-Person POV	*I am swimming.*	*We are swimming.*
Second-Person POV	*You are swimming.*	*You are swimming.*
Third-Person POV	*He is swimming.*	*They are swimming.*

In each example above, the verb agrees with its singular or plural subject.

Words Between Subjects and Verbs

Interrupting words such as *of* and *to* are commonly used between subjects and verbs. For example:

> The lowest point *of* his career was yesterday, when he missed the penalty shot in the playoff game.

The subject here is *lowest point*, and the verb is *was.* Notice how the phrase *of his career* doesn't influence the verb *was.*

Compound Subjects

With a compound subject there's more than one subject (plural), so the verb must be plural. For example:

> *Mike and Vince* play basketball on Friday nights.

Notice how the compound subject (*Mike and Vince*) requires a plural verb (*play*) to agree.

Subjects Joined by *Or* or *Nor*

When singular subjects are joined by the words *or* or *nor*, they require a singular verb. If there are plural subjects, *the subject closest to the verb* determines if the verb is singular or plural. Here are examples of both:

> The table or the couch arrives tomorrow.

The singular verb (*arrives*) is used because the two singular subjects (*table* and *couch*) are joined by the word *or*.

> The table or the *couches* arrive tomorrow.

In this case, the plural verb (*arrive*) is used because the subject closest to the verb (*couches*) is plural.

Indefinite Pronouns *Either, Neither,* and *Each*

In a sentence, the words *either, neither,* and *each* act as singular subjects. For example:

> *Neither* of the printers *is* working properly.

Since the word *neither* acts as a singular subject, the verb (*is*) must also be singular.

The Adjectives *Every* and *Any* with Compounds

Compound words containing the adjectives *every* and *any* (e.g., everybody, anyone) act as singular subjects, so the verb must be singular. For example:

> *Everyone is* here for the surprise party!

Notice how the verb (*is*) is singular because the word *everyone* begins with *every.*

Collective Nouns

Collective nouns represent a group or collection of people, places, or things. Words such as *team, class, family,* and *jury* are all examples of collective nouns. When using a collective noun in a sentence, the verb is singular if the group is working together as a whole. For example:

> Their *family is* waiting for the dog to come home.

The collective noun *family* determines the singular verb *is* instead of *are.* A simple trick would be to replace the collective noun with a pronoun. In this case, replace *Their family* with *it,* since *family* refers to a single unit.

Plural Form and Singular Meaning

Some nouns are naturally plural. The words *acoustics, mathematics,* and *news* are all singular in meaning but plural in form. For plural nouns with singular meaning, the verb is singular. For example:

> The *news is* doing a special on male teachers in elementary education.

Notice how *news* seems plural but is actually singular. Therefore, it uses the singular verb *is.*

Complements

Nouns, pronouns, and adjectives can act as *complements*, providing details to complete the meaning of a sentence. These so-called "sentence completers" include predicate nominatives, predicate adjectives, direct objects, and indirect objects. It's important to note that both predicate nominatives and predicate adjectives follow *linking verbs* (e.g., *is, am, are, was, were, be, being, been*) that show no action.

Predicate Nominatives

Predicate nominatives are nouns or pronouns that rename or modify the subject and *follow a linking verb*. For example:

> My dog is a poodle.

In this sentence, the word *poodle* renames the subject (*dog*) and follows the linking verb (*is*).

Predicate Adjectives

Predicate adjectives are adjectives that rename or modify the subject and *follow a linking verb*. For example:

> My cat is lazy.

In this sentence, the word *lazy* is the predicate adjective because it modifies the subject (*cat*) and follows the linking verb (*is*).

Direct Objects

A *direct object* is a noun, pronoun, or phrase that follows an action verb and answers the question *what* or *who* about the verb. Though a sentence needs a subject and a verb to be complete, it doesn't always need a direct object. To find the direct object in a sentence, look at the following formula:

> Subject + Verb + *what*? or *who*? = Direct Object

Now, apply this formula to the following sentence:

> Spike and Sheena chased the ball around the house.
>
> Subject(s): *Spike and Sheena*
>
> Verb: *chased*
>
> Direct Object: *the ball*

<u>Indirect Objects</u>

An *indirect object* is a noun or pronoun that tells *to whom* or *for whom* the action of the verb is being done. A sentence must have a direct object to have an indirect object. When looking for the indirect object in a sentence, first find the verb and then ask the question *to whom* or *for whom*. For example:

> Lucy passed the crayon to her friend.

In this sentence, the indirect object is *her friend* because it answers *to whom* Lucy *passed* (verb) *the crayon* (direct object).

Pronoun Usage

A *pronoun* is a word that takes the place of a noun. This section looks at the different ways that pronouns are used in sentences.

<u>Pronoun-Antecedent Agreement</u>

An *antecedent* is a word or phrase that typically comes first, followed by a pronoun that refers to it. The pronoun must agree with its antecedent in form (singular or plural). For example:

> *Singular Agreement*:
>
> > The *package* was dropped off at my door, and *it* was very heavy.
>
> Here the antecedent (*package*) is singular, so the pronoun (*it*) must also be singular.
>
> *Plural Agreement*:
>
> > The *packages* were dropped off at my door, and *they* were very heavy.
>
> In this example, the antecedent (*packages*) is plural, so the pronoun (*they*) must also be in plural form.

When there are *compound subjects* (more than one subject) in a sentence, test each pronoun individually with the verb to determine which one is correct. To do this, simply remove the first subject, read the sentence with the remaining pronoun, and decide which one sounds better. For example, look at these two sentences:

> Mom and I are going to the park.
>
> Mom and me are going to the park.

Delete the first subject (*Mom*) from the sentences and then read them both (*I am going to the park* and *me is going to the park*). Which one sounds better? Clearly the first sentence, so the pronoun *I* is the correct choice.

Pronoun Reference

A pronoun shouldn't confuse the reader about whom or what it's describing, and it should clearly refer to its antecedent. For example:

Unclear: The shovel and the pail floated away in the ocean, and it was long gone.

In this sentence, it can't be determined if the pronoun *it* refers to *the shovel* or *the pail*.

Clear: The pail floated away in the ocean, and it was long gone.

In this sentence, the pronoun *it* clearly refers to its antecedent, *the pail*.

Personal Pronouns

Personal pronouns can be in the subjective, objective, or possessive case:

Subjective Case: The pronoun replaces the subject of the sentence.

Objective Case: The pronoun functions as the object.

Possessive Case: The pronoun shows possession of something.

The table below provides examples of each personal pronoun case:

Subjective	Objective	Possessive
I	Me	Mine
You	You	Yours
He	Him	His
She	Her	Hers
It	It	Its
We	Us	Ours
They	Them	Theirs
*Who	*Whom	Whose

*The pronouns *who* and *whom* are often used incorrectly. Use the pronoun *who* when referring to the *subject* of the sentence. Use the pronoun *whom* when referring to the *object* of the sentence.

In the following sentence, identify each pronoun and its case:

The flowers grew in his garden.

The pronoun is *his,* and it's in the possessive case.

Can someone please tell them to turn the music down?

The pronoun is *them,* and it's in the objective case.

Melissa is a really good cook, and she uses only fresh ingredients.

The pronoun is *she,* and it's in the subjective case.

Sentence Structures

There are many ways to organize the words in a sentence to clarify ideas. The four main sentence structures are simple sentences, compound sentences, complex sentences, and compound-complex sentences. In writing, using a variety of these structures makes the style more effective.

Simple Sentences
A *simple sentence* is made up of one independent clause. An *independent clause* is a separate complete thought that can stand on its own, and contains a subject and a predicate. Simple sentences can have compound subjects or compound verbs, but they can only have one main thought. The following is an example of a simple sentence:

> The bus was late.

The singular subject is *bus*, and the predicate is *was late*, so the sentence is a complete thought.

Compound Sentences
A *compound sentence* uses a conjunction to join two independent clauses. *Conjunctions* are linking words such as *and, but, for, nor, or, so,* and *yet*. For example:

> Bradley waited for the bus, but the bus was late.

In this sentence there are two complete thoughts (*Bradley waited for the bus* and *the bus was late*) joined by the conjunction *but*. Therefore, this is a compound sentence.

Complex Sentences
A *complex sentence* consists of one independent clause and one or more dependent clauses. A *dependent clause* is a clause that contains a subject and a verb, but can't stand on its own as a sentence. Complex sentences often use words like *after, although, before, while, wherever, if,* and *since.* For example:

> Although she really enjoyed the opera, Mary was very tired by the end of the night.

The first word in the sentence (*Although*) immediately attracts the reader's attention. The dependent clause (*Although she really enjoyed the opera*) is followed by the independent clause (*Mary was very tired by the end of the night*), which makes this a complex sentence.

Compound-Complex Sentences
A *compound-complex sentence* has at least two independent clauses and at least one dependent clause. For example:

> Although she really enjoyed the opera, Mary was very tired by the end of the night, and she still had to walk home.

The dependent clause (*Although she really enjoyed the opera*) depends on both the first independent clause (*Mary was very tired by the end of the night*) and the second independent clause (*and she still had to walk home*).

Sentence Fragments

A *sentence fragment* is an incomplete sentence that can't stand on its own. It's a dependent clause or phrase that looks like sentences but isn't. A sentence fragment may start with a capital letter and end with punctuation, but it isn't a complete thought. To revise a sentence fragment, either link the fragment to another sentence or add on to create a complete sentence. Look at the following example:

I turned off the television. Because the phone was ringing.

Fragment: *Because the phone was ringing.*

Possible revisions:

I turned off the television because the phone was ringing.

Because the phone was ringing, I ran upstairs to answer it.

Dangling and Misplaced Modifiers

Dangling Modifiers

A *dangling modifier* is a word or phrase where the word it's supposed to modify is missing. In other words, it has nothing to modify. It can also be a dependent clause that's not logically related to the word it should modify. To correct a dangling modifier, connect it to the word it's to modify. For example:

Dangling: Having designed the float for the parade, it will take six months to build it.

Revised: Having designed the float for the parade, he expects to build it in six months.

In the revision, *Having designed* now correctly modifies the subject of the sentence (*he*).

Misplaced Modifiers

A *misplaced modifier* is word or phrase that's separated from the word that it's supposed to modify. Though a modifier can be put in more than one place within a sentence, the modifier should be clearly attached to the word it describes. For example:

Misplaced: The dog almost chased the squirrel for an hour.

Revised: The dog chased the squirrel for almost an hour.

In this example, the dog didn't *almost* chase the squirrel, it *did* chase the squirrel. The revised version of the sentence connects the word *almost* to the words *an hour,* which creates the clearest meaning of the sentence.

Run-On Sentences

A *run-on sentence* has two or more independent clauses that aren't connected by any punctuation. Instead, the sentence goes on and on without any pauses or stops. Here are some ways to correct a run-on sentence:

Add a comma and a coordinating conjunction:

> *Incorrect*: I loaded the dishwasher can you drain the sink?

> *Correct*: I loaded the dishwasher, so can you drain the sink?

Add a semicolon, colon, or dash (without a coordinating conjunction) when the two independent clauses are related to each other:

> *Incorrect*: I went to the movies at the snack bar I bought candy.

> *Correct*: I went to the movies; there I bought candy at the snack bar.

Separate the clauses by turning them into two separate sentences:

> *Incorrect*: The grocery store was busy it quickly sold out of bread.

> *Correct*: The grocery store was busy. It quickly sold out of bread.

Turn one of the independent clauses into a phrase:

> *Incorrect*: The grocery store was busy it quickly sold out of bread.

> *Correct*: The busy grocery store quickly sold out of bread.

Practice Questions

Directions: In each pair of sentences, select the sentence (a or b) that is written most clearly. Keep in mind the basic elements of grammar as they relate to writing clarity.

1.
   a. Detective Shaw and Officer Boyd chases the suspect into the alley so he can't escape.
   b. Detective Shaw and Officer Boyd chase the suspect into the alley so he can't escape.

2.
   a. The jury is still out trying to reach a verdict.
   b. The jury are still out trying to reach a verdict.

3.
   a. The gun or the bullets was taken from the evidence locker without permission.
   b. The gun or the bullets were taken from the evidence locker without permission.

4.
   a. Officer Brady and me returned to the crime scene to interview the witnesses.
   b. Officer Brady and I returned to the crime scene to interview the witnesses.

5.
   a. Neither of the witness statements shows the time of the accident.
   b. Neither of the witness statements show the time of the accident.

6.
   a. The prisoner was able to escape. Because the cell door wasn't locked.
   b. The prisoner was able to escape because the cell door wasn't locked.

7.
   a. Having finished the police report, Officer Grant closed the case.
   b. Having finished the police report, the case was closed.

8.
   a. When the lawyer arrived late to court, the judge had good reason to reprimand her.
   b. The judge had good reason to reprimand the lawyer when she arrived late to court.

9.
   a. Who is taking the suspect downtown for questioning?
   b. Who are taking the suspect downtown for questioning?

10.
   a. The flashing police car's lights could be seen two blocks away.
   b. The police car's flashing lights could be seen two blocks away.

11.
   a. Detective Reid finished collecting evidence at the crime scene. He placed each hair sample and carpet fiber in separate envelopes.
   b. Detective Reid finished collecting evidence at the crime scene he placed each hair sample and carpet fiber in separate envelopes.

12.

    a. In some states, guns injure more people than traffic accidents.

    b. In some states, more people are injured by guns than by traffic accidents.

13.

    a. Not everybody have the honesty, strength, and commitment it takes to become a law enforcement professional.

    b. Not everybody has the honesty, strength, and commitment it takes to become a law enforcement professional.

14.

    a. After graduating from high school, John's father suggested that he apply to the police academy.

    b. After John graduated from high school, his father suggested that he apply to the police academy.

15.

    a. Tonight's news has a story about an officer who apprehended an FBI fugitive during a routine traffic stop.

    b. Tonight's news have a story about an officer who apprehended an FBI fugitive during a routine traffic stop.

Answer Explanations

1. B: This sentence contains a compound subject, which means there's more than one subject (*Detective Shaw* and *Officer Boyd*). In subject-verb agreement, when the subject is plural the verb must also be plural (*chase*).

2. A: The subject (*jury*) is a collective noun and is treated as a singular subject. For proper subject-verb agreement, the singular subject must have a singular verb.

3. B: In proper subject-verb agreement, when two subjects are joined by the words *or* or *nor*, they usually take a singular verb. However, if one of those subjects is plural, *the subject closest to the verb* determines if the verb is singular or plural. Since the plural subject (*bullets*) is closest to the verb, the plural verb (*were*) is used.

4. B: This sentence contains a compound subject (more than one subject). The first subject is a noun (*Officer Brady*), while the second subject is a pronoun (*me* or *I*). To test which pronoun is correct, remove the first subject (*Officer Brady*), read the sentence with each pronoun, and then decide which sentence sounds better. In this case, the pronoun *I* is the best choice, so Choice *B* is correct.

5. A: The words *either*, *neither*, and *each* act as singular subjects in a sentence and therefore take a singular verb. *Neither* is the subject of this sentence, so it must take a singular verb (*shows*).

6. B: The first part of Choice *A* is a complete sentence, but the second part (*Because the cell door wasn't locked.*) is actually a sentence fragment. Though it looks like a sentence, because it begins with a capital letter and ends with punctuation, it is considered a fragment. A fragment is an incomplete sentence that can't stand on its own.

7. A: Choice *B* is an example of a dangling modifier, which is when the word that another word (or phrase) is supposed to modify is missing. In other words, the modifier has nothing to modify. In choice *B*, the *case* didn't finish the police report, a person did. In Choice *A*, by adding the name of the person who performed the action (*Officer Grant*), the dangling modifier is corrected.

8. A: In Choice *B*, it's unclear whether the pronoun *she* is referring to the judge or the lawyer arriving late to court. In Choice *A*, by rewriting the sentence, it becomes clear that *she* is the lawyer.

9. A: When using *that, which*, or *who* as the subject of a sentence, the verb is singular. Choice *A* uses the singular form of the verb (*is*).

10. B: This is an example of a misplaced modifier where a word or phrase is separated from the word that it's supposed to modify. In Choice *A*, the *police* is not what's *flashing,* the lights are. The modifier (*flashing*) should be attached to the word it's supposed to describe (*lights*). In Choice *B*, by moving the modifier, it now correctly modifies the word it should.

11. A: A run-on sentence has two or more independent clauses that aren't connected by punctuation, so the sentence goes on and on. Choice *B* is a run-on sentence because there is no punctuation to break up the independent clauses. By adding a period at the end of the first clause and capitalizing the beginning of the next, the run-on becomes two complete sentences.

12. B: Choice *A* lacks clarity, making it sound as if the *guns* are injuring both *people* and *traffic accidents*. Since *guns* can't injure *traffic accidents*, the sentence must be rewritten with greater clarity as done in Choice *B*.

13. B: Compound words that contain the adjectives *every* and *any* (e.g., <u>every</u>body, <u>any</u>one) are treated as singular subjects, so their verbs must also be singular. Since the word *everybody* is singular, its verb must be singular (*has*) as in Choice *B*.

14. B: In Choice *A* it's not clear who the subject of the introductory clause is, so it's unclear if *John* or *John's father* is the one who graduated from high school. Though the reader could guess what's actually meant, it's better for the sentence to be clear (as in Choice *B*) so there's no confusion about who graduated.

15. A: Some nouns like *news*, *measles*, and *mathematics* are all singular in meaning but plural in form. In this sentence, the word *news* seems plural but is actually singular. These *plural nouns with singular meaning* take a singular verb, so Choice *A* is correct with the use of the singular verb *has*.

Spelling

Police officers are expected to express themselves with authority. Choosing the best words for each situation is only part of this task. Being able to spell those words correctly is also crucial. For this reason, their aptitude for spelling is measured on the California POST. Consider, too, that accurate spelling helps to convey competence and professionalism.

The spelling test portion of the exam includes fifteen multiple-choice items, each featuring a sentence with one word omitted. The answer choices will present four different spellings of the same word, only one of which is correct. Test takers will be asked to identify the correct spelling.

Importance of Prefixes and Suffixes

The most common spelling mistakes are made when a *root word* (or a basic, core word) is modified by adding a prefix or a suffix to it. A *prefix* is a group of letters added to the beginning of a word, and a *suffix* is a group of letters added to the end of a word.

The prefixes usually change the meaning of the word. They might be negative or positive and signal time, location, or number. Note the spelling of the root word (or base word) does not change when adding a prefix.

Common Prefixes		
Prefix	**Meaning**	**Example**
dis-	not, opposite	disagree, disproportionate
en-, em-	to make, to cause	encode, embrace
in-, im-	in, into	induct
ir-, il-, im-	not, opposite	impossible, irresponsible
mis-	bad, wrongly	misfire, mistake
mono-	alone, one	monologue
non-	not, opposite	nonsense
over-	more than, too much	overlook
pre-	before	precede
post-	after	postmortem
re-	again, back	review
un-	not, opposite	unacceptable

A suffix can change the base word in two ways:

- Change numerical agreement: turns a singular word into a plural word (a singular *witness* becomes plural *witnesses*)

- Change grammatical function: turns one part of speech into another (noun to verb, verb to adverb), such as modera*tion,* modera*ting,* or moderate*ly*

Common Suffixes		
Suffix	**Meaning/Use**	**Example**
-able, -ible	able to	unbearable, plausible
-ance	state of being	significance
-al, -ial	relating to	lethal, testimonial, criminal
-ceed, -sede, -cede	go, go forward, withdraw, yield	exceed, recede, supersede
-ed	changes root word to past tense or past participle	called, played
-en	makes root word a verb	heighten, liven
-er	more, action, a person who does an action	clearer, sever, believer
-ful	full of	hateful, beautiful
-ian, -ite	person who does the action, part of a group	politician, meteorite
-ice, -ize	cause, treat, become	service, popularize
-ing	action	writing, playing
-ion, -tion	action or condition	celebration, organization
-ism	forms nouns referring to beliefs or behavior	Buddhism, recidivism
-ity, -ty	state of being	adversity, cruelty
-ive, -tive	state or quality	defensive, conservative
-less	without	tactless, nameless
-ly	in such a manner	poorly, happily
-ment	action	endorsement, disagreement
-ness	makes root word a noun referring to a state of being	weakness, kindness
-or	a person who does an action	moderator, perpetrator
-s, -es	makes root word plural	weights, boxes
-sion	state of being	admission, immersion
-y	made up of	moody, greasy

Doubling-Up Consonants (or Not)
When adding some suffixes (usually, *-ing*, *-sion*) to a root word that ends in one vowel followed immediately by one consonant, *double that last consonant.*

Base Word	**Vowel/consonant**	**Suffix**	**Spelling Change**
wrap	a, p	-ing	wrapping
canvas	a,s		canvassing
admit	i, t	-sion	admission

This rule does not apply to multi-vowel words, such as *sleep*, *treat*, and *appear*. When attaching a suffix that begins with a vowel to a word with a multi-letter vowel followed by a consonant, *do not double the consonant.*

Base Word	Multi-vowel, consonant	Suffix	Spelling
sleep	ee, p	-ing	sleeping
treat	ea, t	-ed	treated
appear	ea, r	-ance	appearance

Do *not* double the consonant if the root word already ends in a double consonant or the letter *x* (examples—*add/adding, fox/foxes*).

Words Ending with *y* or *c*

If a root word ends in a single vowel *y*, the *y* should be changed to *i* when adding any suffix, unless that suffix begins with the letter *i*. If a root word ends in a two-letter vowel, such as *oy, ay,* or *ey*, the *y* is kept.

Root Word	Ending	Suffix	Spelling Change
baby	y	-ed	babied
stymy	y		stymied
crony	y	-ism	cronyism
say	y	-ing	saying
annoy	oy	-ance	annoyance
survey	ey	-ing	surveying

In cases where the root word is a verb (ending with the letter *c*) and the suffix begins with an *e, i,* or *y*, the letter *k* is added to the end of the word between the last letter and the suffix.

Root Word	Ending	Suffix	Spelling Change
panic	ic	-ing	panicking
		-y	panicky
traffic	ic	-ed	trafficked
		-er	trafficker

Words with *ie* or *ei*

There's an old saying "*I* before *E*, except after *C*." There's also a second part to it:

> *I* before *E*,
>
> Except after *C*,
>
> Or when sounded as *A*,
>
> As in *neighbor* and *weigh*.

Here are a few examples:

- *friend, wield, yield* (*i* before *e*)
- *receipt, deceive* (except after *c*)
- *weight, freight* (or when sounded as *a*)

Words Ending in *e*
Generally, the *e* at the end of English words is silent or not pronounced (e.g., *bake*).

- If the suffix being added to a root word begins with a consonant, keep the *e.*
- If the suffix begins with a vowel, the final silent *e* is dropped.

Root Word	Ending	Suffix	Spelling Change
waste remorse pause	silent *e*	-ful -s	wasteful remorseful pauses
reserve pause	silent *e*	-ation -ing	reservation pausing

Exceptions: When the root word ends in *ce* or *ge* and the suffix *–able* or *–ous* is being added, the silent final *e* is kept (e.g., *courageous, noticeable*).

Words Ending with -*ise* or -*ize*
Sometimes, it can be difficult to tell whether a word (usually a verb) should end in *–ise* or *–ize.* In American English, only a few words end with *–ise.* A few examples are *advertise, advise,* and *compromise.* Most words are more likely to end in *–ize.* A few examples are *accessorize, authorize, capitalize,* and *legalize.*

Words Ending with -*ceed*, -*sede*, or -*cede*
It can also be difficult to tell whether a word should end in *–ceed, –sede,* or *–cede.* In the English language, there are only three words that end with *–ceed*: *exceed, proceed,* and *succeed.* There is only one word that ends with *–sede*: *supersede.*

If a word other than *supersede* ends in a suffix that sounds like *–sede,* it should probably be *–cede.* For example: *concede, recede,* and *precede.*

Words Ending in *–able* or *–ible*
In the English language, more words end in *–able* than in *–ible*:

- e.g., *probable, actionable, approachable, traceable*
- e.g., *accessible, admissible, plausible*

<u>Words Ending in -*ance* or -*ence*</u>
The suffixes -*ance* and -*ence* are added to verbs to change them into nouns or adjectives that refer to a state of being. For example, when -*ance* is added to the verb *perform*, *performance* is formed, referring to the act of performing.

Suffix	When to use	Example
-ance, -ancy, -ant	<ul><li>When the root word ends in a *c* that sounds like *k*</li><li>When the root word ends in a hard *g*</li></ul>	<ul><li>significance</li><li>arrogance</li><li>vacancy</li><li>extravagant</li></ul>
-ence, -ency, -ent	<ul><li>When the root word ends in a *c* that sounds like *s*</li><li>When the root word ends in a *g* that sounds like *j*</li></ul>	<ul><li>adolescence</li><li>convergence</li><li>contingency</li><li>convergent</li></ul>

<u>Words Ending in -*tion*, -*sion*, or -*cian*</u>
The suffixes –*tion* and –*sion* are used when forming nouns that refer to the result of a verb. For example, the result of to *abbreviate* something is an *abbreviation*. Likewise, if a person has *compressed* something, then there is a *compression*.

The suffix –*cian* is used when referring to a person who practices something specific. For example, the person who practices *politics* is a *politician.*

<u>Words Containing -*ai* or -*ia*</u>
Unfortunately, there isn't an easy-to-remember rhyme for deciding whether a word containing the vowels *a* and *i* should be spelled *ai* or *ia.* In this case, it's helpful to rely on pronunciation to determine the correct spelling.

The combination of *ai* is one sound, as in the words capt*ai*n and f*ai*nt.

The combination of *ia*, on the other hand, is two separate sounds, as in the words guard*ia*n and d*ia*bolical.

It's helpful to say the word out loud to decide which combination of the two vowels is correct.

Rules for Plural Nouns

<u>Nouns Ending in -*ch*, -*sh*, -*s*, -*x*, or -*z*</u>
When modifying a noun that ends in *ch, sh, s, x,* or *z* to its plural form, add *es* instead of the singular *s.* For example, *trench* becomes *trenches, ash* becomes *ashes, business* becomes *businesses, jukebox* becomes *jukeboxes,* and *fox* becomes *foxes.*

This rule also applies to family names. For example, the Finch family becomes the *Finches,* and the Martinez family becomes the *Martinezes.*

<u>Nouns Ending in *y* or *ay*, *ey*, *iy*, *oy*, or *uy*</u>
When forming plurals with nouns ending in the consonant *y,* the *y* is replaced with *-ies.* For example, *spy* becomes *spies*, and *city* becomes *cities.*

If a noun ends with a vowel before a *y*, the *y* is kept, and an *s* is added. For example, *key* becomes *keys,* and *foray* becomes *forays.*

<u>Nouns Ending in *f* or *fe*</u>
When forming plurals with nouns ending in *f* or *fe,* the *f* is replaced with *v*, and *es* is added. For example, *half* becomes *halves,* and *knife* becomes *knives.*

Some exceptions are *roof/roofs* and *reef/reefs.*

<u>Nouns Ending in *o*</u>
When forming plurals with nouns ending in a consonant and *o*, the *o* is kept and an *es* is added. For example, *tomato* becomes *tomatoes.*

Musical terms are the exception to this rule. Words like *soprano* and *piano* are pluralized by adding *s* even though they end in a consonant and *o* (*sopranos, pianos*).

When forming plurals with nouns ending in a vowel and *o*, the *o* is kept, and *s* is added. For example, *ratio* becomes *ratios,* and *patio* becomes *patios.*

Exceptions to the Rules of Plurals

For some nouns, instead of changing or adding letters at the end of the word, changes to the vowels *within* the words are necessary. For example:

- *man* becomes *men*
- *woman* becomes *women*
- *child* becomes *children*

Some nouns, when pluralized, change entirely:

- *tooth* becomes *teeth*
- *foot* becomes *feet*
- *mouse* becomes *mice*

The opposite is also true; some nouns are the same in the plural as they are in the singular form. For example, *deer, species, fish,* and *sheep* are all plural nouns in singular form.

Practice Questions

Directions: In the following sentences, choose the correct spelling of the missing word. Mark the letter that identifies your choice on the answer sheet.

1. A non-violent breach of a law to bring about social change is called civil _____.
    a. disobidiance.
    b. disobedense.
    c. disobedience.
    d. disobediance.

2. After graduating from the Police Academy, you will be assigned to a _____.
    a. pricinct.
    b. precint.
    c. precinct.
    d. presinct.

3. Becoming a police officer is a great _____ to serve your community.
    a. oppurtinity
    b. opportunity
    c. opportinity
    d. oppurtunity

4. I _____ spilled coffee on my desk.
    a. acidentally
    b. assidentilly
    c. accidentilly
    d. accidentally

5. Your excellent work shows how _____ you are to the job.
    a. comited
    b. comitted
    c. commited
    d. committed

6. My flushed cheeks gave away my _____.
    a. embarassmint.
    b. embarrasment.
    c. embarrissment.
    d. embarrassment.

7. We have the lowest price, _____.
    a. guarenteed.
    b. guaranted.
    c. guarinteed.
    d. guaranteed.

8. Though baseball is my favorite sport, I _____ play golf.
   a. occasionaly
   b. occasionally
   c. ocassionally
   d. occassionaly

9. The *New York Journal* has _____ endorsed Andrew Walter for Congress.
   a. explicitally
   b. explicitly
   c. explicitely
   d. explicately

10. A _____ approach to cooking will ensure that your meals are healthy and delicious.
    a. conscientios
    b. concientious
    c. conscientious
    d. consciencious

11. I'm _____ looking forward to my vacation this year.
    a. definitly
    b. definitely
    c. defenitely
    d. definately

12. I hope that scientists are able to prove the _____ of aliens.
    a. existanse
    b. esixtinse
    c. existense
    d. existence

13. _____ speaking, our operating system is one of the best on the market.
    a. Technicaly
    b. Technicilly
    c. Technically
    d. Technikcally

14. When in need of advice on a case, I consult with my _____.
    a. sergeant.
    b. sergant.
    c. saergant.
    d. seargeant.

15. The car was _____ new when she purchased it.
    a. practicilly
    b. practicaly
    c. practikally
    d. practically

Answer Explanations

1. C

2. C

3. B

4. D

5. D

6. D

7. D

8. B

9. B

10. C

11. B

12. D

13. C

14. A

15. D

Vocabulary

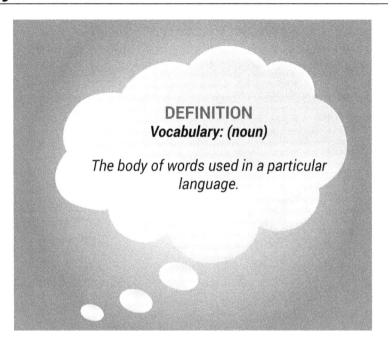

Vocabulary is simply the words a person uses and understands on a daily basis. Having a good vocabulary is important in both written and verbal communications. In law enforcement, officers may have to read court records, police reports, and other legal documents. Many of these materials may contain unfamiliar words, so it's important for officers to learn ways to uncover a word's meaning so they can use it correctly in their own writing.

To understand the challenges of using vocabulary correctly, imagine suddenly being thrust into a foreign country. Not knowing the right words to use when asking for basic necessities (e.g., food, a place to stay, a bathroom) would make everyday life extremely difficult. Asking for help from foreigners who don't share the same vocabulary is hard, since language is what facilitates understanding between people. The more vocabulary words a person understands, the more precisely they can communicate their intentions. This section of the study guide focuses on understanding and deciphering vocabulary through basic grammar.

Prefixes and Suffixes

In the previous section, we went over the particular *spelling* of prefixes and suffixes, and how they changed the root word. In this section, we will look at the *meaning* of various prefixes and suffixes when added to a root word. As mentioned before, a *prefix* is a combination of letters found at the beginning of a word, while a *suffix* is a combination of letters found at the end. A *root word* is the word that comes after the prefix, before the suffix, or between them both. Sometimes a root word can stand on its own without either a prefix or a suffix. More simply put:

Prefix + Root Word = Word

Root Word + Suffix = Word

Prefix + Root Word + Suffix = Word

Root Word = Word

Knowing the definitions of common prefixes and suffixes can help when trying to determine the meaning of an unknown word. In addition, knowing prefixes can help in determining the number of things, the negative of something, or the time and space of an object. Understanding suffix definitions can help when trying to determine the meaning of an adjective, noun, or verb.

The following charts review some of the most common prefixes, what they mean, and how they're used to decipher a word's meaning:

Number and Quantity Prefixes

Prefix	Definition	Example
bi-	two	bicycle, bilateral
mono-	one, single	monopoly, monotone
poly-	many	polygamy, polygon
semi-	half, partly	semiannual, semicircle
uni-	one	unicycle, universal

Here's an example of a number prefix:

The countries signed a *bilateral* agreement; both had to abide by the contract.

Look at the word *bilateral*. If the root word (*lateral*) is unfamiliar, the prefix (*bi-*) can provide a vital clue to its meaning. The prefix *bi-* means *two*, which shows that the agreement involves two of something, most likely the two countries, since *both had to abide by the contract*. This is correct since *bilateral* actually means "involving two parties, usually countries."

Negative Prefixes

Prefix	Definition	Example
a-	without, lack of	amoral, atypical
in-	not, opposing	inability, inverted
non-	not	nonexistent, nonstop
un-	not, reverse	unable, unspoken

Here's an example of a negative prefix:

The patient's *inability* to speak made the doctor wonder what was wrong.

Look at the word *inability.* In the chart above, the prefix *in-* means *not* or *opposing*. By replacing the prefix with *not* and placing it in front of the root word of *ability* (*able*), the meaning of the word becomes clear: *not able*. Therefore, the patient was *not able* to speak.

Time and Space Prefixes

Prefix	Definition	Example
a-	in, on, of, up, to	aloof, associate
ab-	from, away, off	abstract, absent
ad-	to, towards	adept, adjacent
ante-	before, previous	antebellum, antenna
anti-	against, opposing	anticipate, antisocial
cata-	down, away, thoroughly	catacomb, catalogue
circum-	around	circumstance, circumvent
com-	with, together, very	combine, compel
contra-	against, opposing	contraband, contrast
de-	from	decrease, descend
dia-	through, across, apart	diagram, dialect
dis-	away, off, down, not	disregard, disrespect
epi-	upon	epidemic, epiphany
ex-	out	example, exit
hypo-	under, beneath	hypoallergenic, hypothermia
inter-	among, between	intermediate, international
intra-	within	intrapersonal, intravenous
ob-	against, opposing	obtain, obscure
per-	through	permanent, persist
peri-	around	periodontal, periphery
post-	after, following	postdate, postoperative
pre-	before, previous	precede, premeditate
pro-	forward, in place of	program, propel
retro-	back, backward	retroactive, retrofit
sub-	under, beneath	submarine, substantial
super-	above, extra	superior, supersede
trans-	across, beyond, over	transform, transmit
ultra-	beyond, excessively	ultraclean, ultralight

Here's an example of a space prefix:

> The teacher's motivational speech helped *propel* her students toward greater academic achievement.

Look at the word *propel*. The prefix *pro-* means *forward* or *in place of* which indicates something relevant to time and space. *Propel* means to drive or move in a direction (usually forward), so knowing the prefix *pro-* helps interpret that the students are moving forward *toward greater academic achievement*.

Miscellaneous Prefixes

Prefix	Definition	Example
belli-	war, warlike	bellied, belligerent
bene-	well, good	benediction, beneficial
equi-	equal	equidistant, equinox
for-	away, off, from	forbidden, forsaken
fore-	previous	forecast, forebode
homo-	same, equal	homogeneous, homonym
hyper-	excessive, over	hyperextend, hyperactive
in-	in, into	insignificant, invasive
magn-	large	magnetic, magnificent
mal-	bad, poorly, not	maladapted, malnourished
mis-	bad, poorly, not	misplace, misguide
mor-	death	mortal, morgue
neo-	new	neoclassical, neonatal
omni-	all, everywhere	omnipotent, omnipresent
ortho-	right, straight	orthodontist, orthopedic
over-	above	overload, overstock,
pan-	all, entire	panacea, pander
para-	beside, beyond	paradigm, parameter
phil-	love, like	philanthropy, philosophic
prim-	first, early	primal, primer
re-	backward, again	reload, regress
sym-	with, together	symmetry, symbolize
vis-	to see	visual, visibility

Here's another prefix example:

The computer was *primitive*; it still had a floppy disk drive!

The word *primitive* has the prefix *prim-* which indicates being *first* or *early*. *Primitive* means the early stages of evolution or the historical development of something. Therefore, the sentence infers that the computer is an older model because it no longer has a floppy disk drive.

The charts that follow review some of the most common suffixes and include examples of how they're used to determine the meaning of a word. Remember, suffixes are added to the *end* of a root word:

Adjective Suffixes

Suffix	Definition	Example
-able (-ible)	capable of being	teachable, accessible
-esque	in the style of, like	humoresque, statuesque
-ful	filled with, marked by	helpful, deceitful
-ic	having, containing	manic, elastic
-ish	suggesting, like	malnourish, tarnish
-less	lacking, without	worthless, fearless
-ous	marked by, given to	generous, previous

Here's an example of an adjective suffix:

The live model looked so *statuesque* in the window display; she didn't even move!

Look at the word *statuesque*. The suffix *-esque* means *in the style of* or *like*. If something is *statuesque*, it's *in the style of a statue* or *like a statue*. In this sentence, the model looks *like* a statue.

Noun Suffixes

Suffix	Definition	Example
-acy	state, condition	literacy, legacy
-ance	act, condition, fact	distance, importance
-ard	one that does	leotard, billiard
-ation	action, state, result	legislation, condemnation
-dom	state, rank, condition	freedom, kingdom
-er (-or)	office, action	commuter, spectator
-ess	feminine	caress, princess
-hood	state, condition	childhood, livelihood
-ion	action, result, state	communion, position
-ism	act, manner, doctrine	capitalism, patriotism
-ist	worker, follower	stylist, activist
-ity (-ty)	state, quality, condition	community, dirty
-ment	result, action	empowerment, segment
-ness	quality, state	fitness, rudeness
-ship	position	censorship, leadership
-sion (-tion)	state, result	tension, transition
-th	act, state, quality	twentieth, wealth
-tude	quality, state, result	attitude, latitude

Look at the following example of a noun suffix:

The *spectator* cheered when his favorite soccer team scored a goal.

Look at the word *spectator*. The suffix *-or* means *action*. In this sentence, the *action* is to *spectate* (watch something), thus a *spectator* is someone involved in watching something.

Verb Suffixes

Suffix	Definition	Example
-ate	having, showing	facilitate, integrate
-en	cause to be, become	frozen, written
-fy	make, cause to have	modify, rectify
-ize	cause to be, treat with	realize, sanitize

Here's an example of a verb suffix:

The preschool had to *sanitize* the toys every Tuesday and Thursday.

In the word *sanitize*, the suffix *-ize* means *cause to be* or *treat with*. By adding the suffix *-ize* to the root word *sanitary*, the meaning of the word becomes active: *cause to be sanitary*.

Context Clues

It's common to encounter unfamiliar words in written communication. When faced with an unknown word, there are certain "tricks" that can be used to uncover its meaning. *Context clues* are words or phrases within a sentence or paragraph that provide hints about a word and its definition. For example, if an unfamiliar word is anchored to a noun with other attached words as clues, these can help decipher the word's meaning. Consider the following example:

After the treatment, Grandma's natural rosy cheeks looked *wan* and ghostlike.

The unfamiliar word is *wan*. The first clue to its meaning is in the phrase *After the treatment,* which implies that something happened after a procedure (possibly medical). A second clue is the word *rosy*, which describes Grandma's natural cheek color that changed after the treatment. Finally, the word *ghostlike* infers that Grandma's cheeks now look white. By using the context clues in the sentence, the meaning of the word *wan* (which means *pale*) can be deciphered.

Below are some additional ways to use context clues to uncover the meaning of an unknown word:

Contrasts
Look for context clues that *contrast* the unknown word. When reading a sentence with an unfamiliar word, look for a contrasting or opposing word or idea. Here's an example:

Since Mary didn't cite her research sources, she lost significant points for *plagiarizing* the content of her report.

In this sentence, *plagiarizing* is the unfamiliar word. Notice that when Mary *didn't cite her research sources,* it resulted in her losing points for *plagiarizing the content of her report.* These contrasting ideas infer that Mary did something wrong with the content. This makes sense because the definition of *plagiarizing* is "taking the work of someone else and passing it off as your own."

Contrasts often use words like *but, however, although,* or phrases like *on the other hand.* For example:

The *gargantuan* television won't fit in my car, but it will cover the entire wall in the den.

The unfamiliar word is *gargantuan*. Notice that the television is too big to fit in a car, <u>but</u> *it will cover the entire wall in the den*. This infers that the television is extremely large, which is correct, since the word *gargantuan* means "enormous."

<u>Synonyms</u>
Another method is to brainstorm possible synonyms for the unknown word. *Synonyms* are words with the same or similar meanings (e.g., *strong* and *sturdy*). To do this, substitute synonyms one at a time, reading the sentence after each to see if the meaning is clear. By replacing an unknown word with a known one, it may be possible to uncover its meaning. For example:

Gary's clothes were *saturated* after he fell into the swimming pool.

In this sentence, the word *saturated* is unknown. To brainstorm synonyms for *saturated*, think about what happens to Gary's clothes after falling into the swimming pool. They'd be *soaked* or *wet*, both of which turn out to be good synonyms to try since the actual meaning of *saturated* is "thoroughly soaked."

<u>Antonyms</u>
Sometimes sentences contain words or phrases that oppose each other. Opposite words are known as *antonyms* (e.g., *hot* and *cold*). For example:

Although Mark seemed *tranquil*, you could tell he was actually nervous as he paced up and down the hall.

The unknown word here is *tranquil*. The sentence says that Mark was in fact not *tranquil* but was instead *actually nervous*. The opposite of the word *nervous* is *calm*, which is the meaning of the word *tranquil*.

<u>Explanations or Descriptions</u>
Explanations or *descriptions* of other things in the sentence can also provide clues to an unfamiliar word. Take the following example:

Golden Retrievers, Great Danes, and Pugs are the top three *breeds* competing in the dog show.

If the word *breeds* is unknown, look at the sentence for an explanation or description that provides a clue. The subjects (*Golden Retrievers*, *Great Danes*, and *Pugs*) describe different types of dogs. This description helps uncover the meaning of the word *breeds* which is "a particular type or group of animals."

<u>Inferences</u>
Sometimes there are clues to an unknown word that infer or suggest its meaning. These *inferences* can be found either within the sentence where the word appears or in a sentence that precedes or follows it. Look at the following example:

The *wretched* old lady was kicked out of the restaurant. She was so mean and nasty to the waiter!

Here the word *wretched* is unknown. The first sentence states that the *old lady was kicked out of the restaurant*, but it doesn't say why. The sentence that follows tells us why: *She was so mean and nasty to the waiter!* This infers that the old lady was *kicked out* because she was *so mean and nasty* or, in other words, *wretched*.

When preparing for a vocabulary test, try reading challenging materials to learn new words. If a word on the test is unfamiliar, look for prefixes and suffixes to help uncover what the word means and eliminate incorrect answers. If two answers both seem right, determine if there are any differences between them and then select the word that best fits. Context clues in the sentence or paragraph can also help to uncover the meaning of an unknown word. By learning new vocabulary words, a person can expand their knowledge base and improve the quality and effectiveness of their written communications.

Practice Questions

Directions: Read each sentence carefully and select the answer that is closest in meaning to the underlined word. Use prefix/suffix definitions and context clues to help eliminate incorrect answers.

1. Only one of the thieves who robbed the jewelry store was caught since his <u>accomplice</u> got away.
    a. Roommate
    b. Brother
    c. Partner
    d. Manager

2. The congressman denied the <u>allegation</u> that he'd voted in favor of the bill in exchange for a campaign donation.
    a. Claim
    b. Reptile
    c. Highway
    d. Interrogation

3. During the <u>arraignment</u> in front of the judge, Tommy pleaded not guilty to driving under the influence of alcohol.
    a. Wedding
    b. Proceeding
    c. Bouquet
    d. Conclusion

4. The violent offender was convicted of <u>battery</u> for using a baseball bat to strike his victim.
    a. Voltage
    b. Assault
    c. Flattery
    d. Arson

5. The gang members in Shelly's neighborhood tried to <u>coerce</u> her into selling drugs, but she refused to be bullied.
    a. Pay
    b. Discourage
    c. Gender
    d. Pressure

6. The company treasurer was found guilty of <u>embezzling</u> $50,000 from the company's bank account to pay for the remodeling of his home.
    a. Bedazzling
    b. Stealing
    c. Decorating
    d. Borrowing

7. The judge <u>exonerated</u> Susan of all charges, so she left the courtroom a free woman.
   a. Cleared
   b. Executed
   c. Tried
   d. Convicted

8. When officers arrived on the scene of the deadly crash, they learned there had been one <u>fatality</u>.
   a. Birth
   b. Attraction
   c. Death
   d. Celebration

9. The unsuspecting art collector didn't realize the painting was a <u>forgery</u> until after it was appraised, so she became the 13th victim of the con artist.
   a. Antique
   b. Operation
   c. Sculpture
   d. Fake

10. The criminals wore gloves so they wouldn't leave behind any <u>latent</u> fingerprints.
    a. Hidden
    b. Painted
    c. Vinyl
    d. Visible

11. The state declared a <u>moratorium</u> on executions after new evidence cleared one death row inmate of his crime.
    a. Funeral
    b. Postponement
    c. Speech
    d. Hospitalization

12. The witness said the <u>perpetrator</u> wore a black ski mask and a blonde wig during the home invasion.
    a. Model
    b. Student
    c. Criminal
    d. Dancer

13. Though Miss Johnson swore to tell the truth under oath, she actually tried to <u>prevaricate</u> and claimed she didn't remember any details.
    a. Steal
    b. Impregnate
    c. Lie
    d. Confess

14. The city's first responders must follow <u>protocol</u> when handling calls for cases of domestic violence.
    a. Guidelines
    b. Internist
    c. Requests
    d. Evidence

15. After the riot broke out, officers had to use strong measures to <u>quell</u> the angry crowd.
    a. Wave
    b. Count
    c. Incite
    d. Calm

Answer Explanations

1. C: *Partner*: a person who takes part in a plan with another or other persons

Accomplice: a person who joins another person in the act of carrying out a plan (most likely an illegal or unethical one)

2. A: *Claim*: a declaration that something is the truth without the accompaniment of evidence

Allegation: a claim or assertion of some wrongdoing, typically made without proof

3. B: *Proceeding*: the steps of carrying out the law within an institution

Arraignment: the courtroom proceeding where a defendant is apprised of the charges against them and enters a plea of guilty or not guilty

4. B: *Assault*: to attack suddenly and unlawfully

Battery: an assault where the assailant makes physical contact with another person

5. D: *Pressure*: to influence someone to do a particular thing

Coerce: to persuade an unwilling person to do something by using pressure, intimidation, or threats

6. B: *Stealing*: the act of taking a thing from somebody that isn't one's own

Embezzling: to defraud someone or to steal property (often money) entrusted into one's care

7. A: *Cleared*: to be absolved of misunderstanding or doubt

Exonerated: to be pronounced not guilty of criminal charges

8. C: *Death*: the event of a person's life ending

Fatality: a death that occurs as the result of an accident, disaster, war, or disease

9. D: *Fake*: an imitation of reality; a simulation

Forgery: to create or imitate something (e.g., an object or document) with the intent to deceive others or profit from the sale of it

10. A: *Hidden*: something kept out of sight or concealed

Latent: a thing that's hidden, or something that exists but hasn't been developed yet

11. B: *Postponement*: to hold off on a scheduled activity until a later date

Moratorium: a legal postponement or waiting period set by some authority to suspend activity

12. C: *Criminal*: someone who is guilty of a crime

Perpetrator: the person who commits a crime

13. C: *Lie*: to state a contradiction of the truth; to deceive

Prevaricate: to deliberately evade the truth or lie in order to mislead

14. A: *Guidelines*: a set of standards created for a future action

Protocol: official guidelines or procedures that must be followed

15. D: *Calm*: to make tranquil or serene

Quell: to calm, quiet, or put an end to something

Reading Comprehension

Types of Passages

Writing can be classified under four passage types: narrative, expository, technical, and persuasive. Though these types are not mutually exclusive, one form tends to dominate the rest. By recognizing the *type* of passage you're reading, you gain insight into *how* you should read. If you're reading a narrative, you can assume the author intends to entertain, which means you may skim the text without losing meaning. A technical document might require a close read, because skimming the passage might cause the reader to miss salient details.

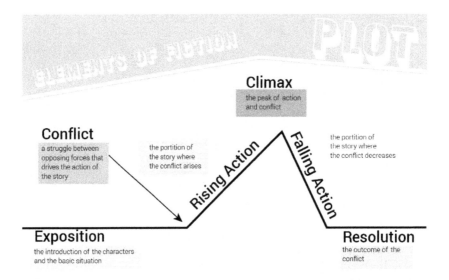

1. *Narrative* writing, at its core, is the art of storytelling. For a narrative to exist, certain elements must be present. It must have characters. While many characters are human, characters could be defined as anything that thinks, acts, and talks like a human. For example, many recent movies, such as *Lord of the Rings* and *The Chronicles of Narnia*, include animals, fantastical creatures, and even trees that behave like humans. It must have a plot or sequence of events. Typically, those events follow a standard plot diagram, but recent trends start *in medias res* or in the middle (near the climax). In this instance, foreshadowing and flashbacks often fill in plot details. Along with characters and a plot, there must also be conflict. Conflict is usually divided into two types: internal and external. Internal conflict indicates the character is in turmoil. Internal conflicts are presented through the character's thoughts. External conflicts are visible. Types of external conflict include person versus person, person versus nature, person versus technology, person versus the supernatural, or a person versus fate.

2. *Expository* writing is detached and to the point, while other types of writing—persuasive, narrative, and descriptive—are lively. Since expository writing is designed to instruct or inform, it usually involves directions and steps written in second person ("you" voice) and lacks any persuasive or narrative elements. Sequence words such as *first*, *second*, and *third*, or *in the first place*, *secondly*, and *lastly* are often given to add fluency and cohesion. Common examples of expository writing include instructor's lessons, cookbook recipes, and repair manuals.

3. Due to its empirical nature, *technical* writing is filled with steps, charts, graphs, data, and statistics. The goal of technical writing is to advance understanding in a field through the scientific method.

Experts such as teachers, doctors, or mechanics use words unique to the profession in which they operate. These words, which often incorporate acronyms, are called *jargon*. Technical writing is a type of expository writing but is not meant to be understood by the general public. Instead, technical writers assume readers have received a formal education in a particular field of study, and need no explanation as to what the jargon means. Imagine a doctor trying to understand a diagnostic reading for a car or a mechanic trying to interpret lab results. Only professionals with proper training will fully comprehend the text.

4. *Persuasive* writing is designed to change opinions and attitudes. The topic, stance, and arguments are found in the thesis, positioned near the end of the introduction. Later supporting paragraphs offer relevant quotations, paraphrases, and summaries from primary or secondary sources, which are then interpreted, analyzed, and evaluated. The goal of persuasive writers is not to stack quotes, but to develop original ideas by using sources as a starting point. Good persuasive writing makes powerful arguments with valid sources and thoughtful analysis. Poor persuasive writing is riddled with bias and logical fallacies. Sometimes, logical and illogical arguments are sandwiched together in the same text. Therefore, readers should display skepticism when reading persuasive arguments.

Organization of the Text

Depending on what the author is attempting to accomplish, certain formats or text structures work better than others. For example, a sequence structure might work for narration but not when identifying similarities and differences between dissimilar concepts. Similarly, a comparison-contrast structure is not useful for narration. It's the author's job to put the right information in the correct format.

Readers should be familiar with the five main literary structures:

1. *Sequence* structure (sometimes referred to as the order structure) is when the order of events proceeds in a predictable order. In many cases, this means the text goes through the plot elements: exposition, rising action, climax, falling action, and resolution. Readers are introduced to characters, setting, and conflict in the exposition. In the rising action, there's an increase in tension and suspense. The climax is the height of tension and the point of no return. Tension decreases during the falling action. In the resolution, any conflicts presented in the exposition are resolved, and the story concludes. An informative text that is structured sequentially will often go in order from one step to the next.

2. In the *problem-solution* structure, authors identify a potential problem and suggest a solution. This form of writing is usually divided into two paragraphs and can be found in informational texts. For example, cell phone, cable, and satellite providers use this structure in manuals to help customers troubleshoot or identify problems with services or products.

3. When authors want to discuss similarities and differences between separate concepts, they arrange thoughts in a *comparison-contrast* paragraph structure. Venn diagrams are an effective graphic organizer for comparison-contrast structures, because they feature two overlapping circles that can be used to organize similarities and differences. A comparison-contrast essay organizes one paragraph based on similarities and another based on differences. A comparison-contrast essay can also be arranged with the similarities and differences of individual traits addressed within individual paragraphs. Words such as *however*, *but*, and *nevertheless* help signal a contrast in ideas.

4. *Descriptive* writing structure is designed to appeal to your senses. Much like an artist who constructs a painting, good descriptive writing builds an image in the reader's mind by appealing to the five senses:

sight, hearing, taste, touch, and smell. However, overly descriptive writing can become tedious; likewise, sparse descriptions can make settings and characters seem flat. Good authors strike a balance by applying descriptions only to passages, characters, and settings that are integral to the plot.

5. Passages that use the *cause and effect* structure are simply asking *why* by demonstrating some type of connection between ideas. Words such as *if, since, because, then,* or *consequently* indicate relationship. By switching the order of a complex sentence, the writer can rearrange the emphasis on different clauses. Saying *If Sheryl is late, we'll miss the dance* is different from saying *We'll miss the dance if Sheryl is late*. One emphasizes Sheryl's tardiness while the other emphasizes missing the dance. Paragraphs can also be arranged in a cause and effect format. Since the format — before and after — is sequential, it is useful when authors wish to discuss the impact of choices. Researchers often apply this paragraph structure to the scientific method.

Purposes for Writing

When it comes to authors' writings, readers should always identify a position or stance. No matter how objective a text may seem, assume the author has preconceived beliefs. Reduce the likelihood of accepting an invalid argument by looking for multiple articles on the topic, including those with varying opinions. If several opinions point in the same direction, and are backed by reputable peer-reviewed sources, it's more likely the author has a valid argument. Positions that run contrary to widely held beliefs and existing data should invite scrutiny. There are exceptions to the rule, so be a careful consumer of information. Though themes, symbols, and motifs are buried deep within the text and can sometimes be difficult to infer, an author's purpose is usually obvious from the beginning.

No matter the genre or format, authors write to persuade, inform, entertain, or express feelings. Often, these purposes are blended, with one dominating the rest. It's useful to learn to recognize the author's intent.

As mentioned before in the *Types of Passages* section, authors use persuasive writing to convince readers of something. It often contains two elements: the argument and the counterargument. The argument takes a stance on an issue, while the counterargument pokes holes in the opposition's stance. Authors rely on logic (logos), emotion (pathos), and credibility (ethos) to persuade readers to agree with them. If readers are opposed to the stance before reading, they are unlikely to adopt that stance. Those who are undecided or committed to the same stance are more likely to agree with the author.

Authors use informative writing to teach or inform. Informative writing includes technical writing or expository writing, as detailed before. Workplace manuals, instructor lessons, statistical reports and cookbooks are examples of informative texts. Informative writing is usually based on facts and is often void of emotion or persuasion. Informative texts likely contain statistics, charts, and graphs. Though most informative texts lack a persuasive agenda, readers must examine the text carefully to determine whether one exists within a given passage.

Authors use stories or narratives with the intent to entertain. When you go to the movies, you often want to escape for a few hours, not necessarily to think critically. Entertaining writing is designed to delight and engage the reader. However, sometimes this type of writing can be woven into more serious material, such as persuasive or informative writing, to hook the reader before transitioning into a more scholarly discussion.

Finally, emotional writing works to evoke the reader's feelings, such as anger, euphoria, or sadness. The connection between reader and author is an attempt to cause the reader to share the author's intended emotion or tone. Sometimes, the author simply wants readers to feel what they felt in order to make the text more poignant. Other times, the author attempts to persuade or manipulate the reader into adopting their stance. While it's okay to sympathize with the author, be aware of the individual's underlying intent.

Writing Devices

Authors utilize a wide range of devices to tell a story or communicate information. Readers should be familiar with the most common of these devices. Writing devices are also commonly known as *techniques of writing* or *rhetorical devices*.

<u>Types of Appeals</u>
In non-fiction writing, authors employ argumentative techniques to present their opinion to readers in the most convincing way. First of all, persuasive writing usually includes at least one type of appeal: an appeal to logic (logos), emotion (pathos), or credibility and trustworthiness (ethos). When a writer appeals to logic, they are asking readers to agree with them based on research, evidence, and an established line of reasoning. An author's argument might also appeal to readers' emotions, perhaps by including personal stories and anecdotes (a short narrative of a specific event). A final type of appeal, appeal to authority, asks the reader to agree with the author's argument on the basis of their expertise or credentials. Consider three different approaches to arguing the same opinion:

Logic (Logos)
> Our school should abolish its current ban on cell phone use on campus. This rule was adopted last year as an attempt to reduce class disruptions and help students focus more on their lessons. However, since the rule was enacted, there has been no change in the number of disciplinary problems in class. Therefore, the rule is ineffective and should be done away with.

The above is an example of an appeal to logic. The author uses evidence to disprove the logic of the school's rule (the rule was supposed to reduce discipline problems; the number of problems has not been reduced; therefore, the rule is not working) and call for its repeal.

Emotion (Pathos)
An author's argument might also appeal to readers' emotions, perhaps by including personal stories and anecdotes.

The next example presents an appeal to emotion. By sharing the personal anecdote of one student and speaking about emotional topics like family relationships, the author invokes the reader's empathy in asking them to reconsider the school rule.

> Our school should abolish its current ban on cell phone use on campus. If they aren't able to use their phones during the school day, many students feel isolated from their loved ones. For example, last semester, one student's grandmother had a heart attack in the morning. However, because he couldn't use his cell phone, the student didn't know about his grandmother's accident until the end of the day—when she had already passed away and it was too late to say goodbye. By preventing students from contacting their friends and family, our school is placing undue stress and anxiety on students.

Credibility (Ethos)
Finally, an appeal to authority includes a statement from a relevant expert. In this case, the author uses a doctor in the field of education to support the argument. All three examples begin from the same

opinion—the school's phone ban needs to change—but rely on different argumentative styles to persuade the reader.

> Our school should abolish its current ban on cell phone use on campus. According to Dr. Bartholomew Everett, a leading educational expert, "Research studies show that cell phone usage has no real impact on student attentiveness. Rather, phones provide a valuable technological resource for learning. Schools need to learn how to integrate this new technology into their curriculum." Rather than banning phones altogether, our school should follow the advice of experts and allow students to use phones as part of their learning.

Rhetorical Questions
Another commonly used argumentative technique is asking rhetorical questions, questions that do not actually require an answer but that push the reader to consider the topic further.

> I wholly disagree with the proposal to ban restaurants from serving foods with high sugar and sodium contents. Do we really want to live in a world where the government can control what we eat? I prefer to make my own food choices.

Here, the author's rhetorical question prompts readers to put themselves in a hypothetical situation and imagine how they would feel about it.

Figurative Language
Simile and *metaphor* are part of figurative language and are used as rhetorical devices. Both are comparisons between two things, but their formats differ slightly. A simile says that two things are *similar* and makes a comparison using *like* or *as*—A is like B, or A is as [some characteristic] as B—whereas a metaphor states that two things are exactly the same—A is B. In both cases, simile and metaphor invite the reader to think more deeply about the characteristics of the two subjects and consider where they overlap. An example of a metaphor would be Shakespeare's line "Juliette is the sun," where Romeo compares Juliette's radiance directly to the sun. For an example of simile, look at the first line of Robert Burns' famous poem:

> My love is like a red, red rose

This is comparison using *like*, and the two things being compared are love and a rose. Some characteristics of a rose are that it is fragrant, beautiful, blossoming, colorful, vibrant—by comparing his love to a red, red rose, Burns asks the reader to apply these qualities of a rose to his love. In this way, he implies that his love is also fresh, blossoming, and brilliant.

Point of View
Point of view is an important writing device to consider. In fiction writing, point of view refers to who tells the story or from whose perspective readers are observing as they read. In non-fiction writing, the *point of view* refers to whether the author refers to themself, the readers, or chooses not to refer to either. Whether fiction or nonfiction, the author will carefully consider the impact the perspective will have on the purpose and main point of the writing.

- First-person point of view: The story is told from the writer's perspective. In fiction, this would mean that the main character is also the narrator. First-person point of view is easily recognized by the use of personal pronouns such as *I, me, we, us, our, my,* and *myself.*

- Third-person point of view: In a more formal essay, this would be an appropriate perspective because the focus should be on the subject matter, not the writer or the reader. Third-person point of view is recognized by the use of the pronouns *he, she, they*, and *it*. In fiction writing, third person point of view has a few variations.

  o *Third-person limited* point of view refers to a story told by a narrator who has access to the thoughts and feelings of just one character.

  o In *third-person omniscient* point of view, the narrator has access to the thoughts and feelings of all the characters.

  o In *third-person objective* point of view, the narrator is like a fly on the wall and can see and hear what the characters do and say, but does not have access to their thoughts and feelings.

- Second-person point of view: This point of view isn't commonly used in fiction or non-fiction writing because it directly addresses the reader using the pronouns *you, your*, and *yourself*. Second-person perspective is more appropriate in direct communication, such as business letters or emails.

Point of View	Pronouns used
First person	I, me, we, us, our, my, myself
Second person	You, your, yourself
Third person	He, she, it, they

Understanding a Passage

In order to understand any text, readers first need to determine what the text is about. In non-fiction writing, the text's *topic* is the most general answer to the question, "What is the writer talking about?" The topic can generally be expressed in just a few words. For example, a passage might be about college education, moving to a new neighborhood, or dog breeds. These are all examples of topics. Slightly more specific information is found in the *main idea*. The main idea answers the question, "What does the writer want readers to know about the topic?" One article might be about the history of popular dog breeds; another article might tell how certain dog breeds are unfairly stereotyped. In both cases, the topic is the same—dog breeds—but the main ideas are quite different. Each writer has a distinct purpose for writing and a different set of details for what they want us to know *about* dog breeds. Whereas the topic can usually be expressed in just a few words, the main idea can be explained in a full sentence. When a writer expresses their main idea in one sentence, this is also known as a *thesis statement* or thesis sentence. If a writer uses a thesis statement, it can generally be found at the beginning of the passage. Finally, the most specific information in a text is in its *supporting details*. To go back to the example of dog breeds, an article about dog breed stereotyping might discuss a case study of pit bulls and provide statistics about how many dog attacks are caused by pit bulls versus other breeds. This specific information that supports the main idea is known as a text's supporting details.

In contrast to informative writing, literary texts contain *themes*. A theme is a very general way to describe the ideas and questions raised in a piece of literature. Like a topic, a theme can often be expressed in just one word or a few words. However, due to the complex nature of literature, most texts contain more than one theme. Some examples of literary themes include isolation, sacrifice, or vengeance. A text's theme might also explore the relationship between two contrasting ideas: ignorance versus knowledge, nature versus technology, science versus religion. From these examples, it should be apparent that a theme generally expresses a relatively broad and abstract idea about the text—so don't confuse a text's theme with its subject. Both theme and subject can answer the question, "What is the story about?" but the subject answers the question in a concrete way whereas the theme answers it in a more abstract way. For example, the subject of *Hamlet* is Hamlet's investigation of his father's murder (a concrete idea of what happens in the story). However, its themes—that is, the ideas explored through the story—include indecision and revenge (fundamental concepts that unite the events of the story). Because the theme is usually abstract, it might seem difficult to identify. Readers can ask themselves several questions as they read to get a better idea of the theme:

- What observations does the writer make about human behavior?
- How do the specific events of this story relate to society in general?
- What forces drive the characters' actions and decisions?
- How did characters change or what did they learn during the story?

Again, remember that the theme generally refers to "big picture" ideas about the story, rather than a specific description of the story's events.

Evaluating a Passage

Readers draw *conclusions* about what an author has presented. This helps them better understand what the writer has intended to communicate and whether they agree with what the author has offered. There are a few ways to determine a logical conclusion, but careful reading is the most important. It's helpful to read a passage a few times, noting details that seem important to the text. Sometimes, readers arrive at a conclusion that is different than what the writer intended or come up with more than one conclusion.

Textual evidence within the details helps readers draw a conclusion about a passage. *Textual evidence* refers to information—facts and examples that support the main point. Textual evidence will likely come from outside sources and can be in the form of quoted or paraphrased material. In order to draw a conclusion from evidence, it's important to examine the credibility and validity of that evidence as well as how (and if) it relates to the main idea.

If an author presents a differing opinion or a counterargument in order to refute it, the reader should consider how and why this information is being presented. It is meant to strengthen the original argument and shouldn't be confused with the author's intended conclusion, but it should also be considered in the reader's final evaluation.

Summarizing is an effective way to draw a conclusion from a passage. A summary is a shortened version of the original text, written by the reader in their own words. Focusing on the main points of the original text and including only the relevant details can help readers reach a conclusion. It's important to retain the original meaning of the passage.

Like summarizing, *paraphrasing* can also help a reader fully understand different parts of a text. Paraphrasing calls for the reader to take a small part of the passage and list or describe its main points. Paraphrasing is more than rewording the original passage, though. It should be written in the reader's own words, while still retaining the meaning of the original source. This will indicate an understanding of the original source, yet still help the reader expand on their interpretation.

Responding to a Passage

There are a few ways for readers to engage actively with the text, such as making inferences and predictions. An *inference*, as mentioned earlier, refers to a point that is implied (as opposed to directly stated) by the evidence presented:

> Bradley packed up all of the items from his desk in a box and said goodbye to his coworkers for the last time.

From this sentence, though it is not directly stated, readers can infer that Bradley is leaving his job. It's necessary to use inference in order to draw conclusions about the meaning of a passage. When making an inference about a passage, it's important to rely only on the information that is provided in the text itself. This helps readers ensure that their conclusions are valid.

Readers will also find themselves making predictions when reading a passage or paragraph. *Predictions* are guesses about what's going to happen next. This is a natural tendency, especially when reading a good story or watching a suspenseful movie. It's fun to try to figure out how it will end. Authors intentionally use suspenseful language and situations to keep readers interested:

> A cat darted across the street just as the car came careening around the curve.

One unfortunate prediction might be that the car will hit the cat. Of course, predictions aren't always accurate, so it's important to read carefully to the end of the text to determine the accuracy of predictions.

Readers should pay attention to the *sequence*, or the order in which details are laid out in the text, as this can be important to understanding its meaning as a whole. Writers will often use transitional words to help the reader understand the order of events and to stay on track. Words like *next, then, after*, and *finally* show that the order of events is important to the author. In some cases, the author omits these transitional words, and the sequence is implied. Authors may even purposely present the information out of order to make an impact or have an effect on the reader. An example might be when a narrative writer uses *flashback* to reveal information.

Drawing conclusions is also important when actively reading a passage. *Hedge phrases* such as *will, might, probably*, and *appear to be* are used by writers who want to cover their bases and make sure to show there are exceptions to their statements. *Absolute phrasing*, such as *always* and *never*, should be carefully considered as they are often incorrect.

Critical Thinking Skills

It's important to read any text critically. The goal is to discover the point and purpose of what the author is writing about through analysis. It's also crucial to establish the point or stance the author has taken on the topic of the text. After determining the author's perspective, readers can then more effectively develop their own viewpoints on the subject of the text.

It is important to distinguish between *fact* and *opinion* when reading a text. When an author presents facts, such as statistics or data, readers should be able to check those facts and make sure they are accurate. When authors use opinion, they are sharing their own thoughts and feelings about a subject.

Authors often use words like *think, feel, believe,* or *in my opinion* when expressing opinion, but these words won't always appear in an opinion piece, especially if it is formally written. An author's opinion may be backed up by facts, which gives it more credibility, but that opinion should not be taken as fact. A critical reader should be suspect of an author's opinion, especially if it is only supported by other opinions.

Fact	Opinion
There are nine innings in a game of baseball.	Baseball games run too long.
Abraham Lincoln was assassinated on April 14, 1865.	Abraham Lincoln should never have been assassinated.
McDonalds has stores in 118 countries.	McDonalds has the best hamburgers.

Critical readers examine the facts used to support an author's argument. They check the facts against other sources to be sure those facts are correct. They also check the validity of the sources used to be sure those sources are credible, academic, and/or peer reviewed. Consider that when an author uses another person's opinion to support their argument, even if it is an expert's opinion, it is still only an opinion and should not be taken as fact. A strong argument uses valid, measurable facts to support ideas. Even then, the reader may disagree with the argument, as it may be rooted in personal beliefs.

An authoritative argument may use the facts to sway the reader. Take for example an argument about global warming. Many experts differ in their opinions of what alternative fuels can be used to aid in offsetting it. Because of this, a writer may choose to only use the information and expert opinion that supports their own viewpoint.

If the argument is that wind energy is the best solution, the author will use facts that support this idea. That same author may leave out relevant facts on solar energy. The way the author uses facts can influence the reader, so it's important to consider the facts being used, how those facts are being presented, and what information might be left out.

Critical readers should also look for errors in the argument such as logical fallacies and bias. A *logical fallacy* is a flaw in the logic used to make the argument. An example would be to rely on thinking that an event could potentially lead to a series of different, increasingly catastrophic events (*slippery slope fallacy*). For example, an author might want to assert that the obesity epidemic is the result of school lunch programs:

> School lunches don't offer healthy options. Kids eat these lunches every day, leading to weight gain. This weight gain can lead to obesity, so schools are to blame for the obesity epidemic.

This argument doesn't take into account the other factors that are at play here. Kids may not eat school lunch every day. It only accounts for one meal of the day for most kids. Even if the food is unhealthy, does the amount eaten factor in to weight gain? If the author can't prove with clear evidence that school lunches are actually leading to weight gain that the obesity epidemic stems from, their logic becomes mere speculation and is flawed.

Authors can also reflect *bias* if they ignore an opposing viewpoint or present their side in an unbalanced way. A strong argument considers the opposition and finds a way to refute it. Critical readers should look for an unfair or one-sided presentation of the argument and be skeptical, as a bias may be present. Even if this bias is unintentional, if it exists in the writing, the reader should be wary of the validity of the argument.

Readers should also look for the use of *stereotypes,* which refer to specific groups. Stereotypes are often negative connotations about a person or place and should always be avoided. When a critical reader finds stereotypes in a text, they should immediately be critical of the argument and consider the validity of anything the author presents. Stereotypes reveal a flaw in the writer's thinking and may suggest a lack of knowledge or understanding about the subject.

Practice Questions

Questions 1 and 2 are based on the following passage:

The majority of records that are taken as part of court proceedings are considered part of the public domain, and are therefore available to anyone who requests access. These documents can be used to conduct background checks, revealing information such as age, marital status, military status, and whether a person has ever been convicted of a crime. While many records are made public, some are sealed by a judge for extraordinary circumstances, such as to protect the privacy of a minor. Each state has its own rules governing which records can be accessed and counties determine how. In some cases the records can be obtained through a quick search of a state or county database, but others will require a request of the appropriate department. For example, in the state of California, most court records can be accessed through county court databases, but supreme and appellate court records are only available from the Appellate Court.

1. Based on the preceding passage, which of the following statements is most accurate?
    a. All court records can be accessed via online databases.
    b. Court records are always part of the public domain, so they can be accessed by anyone.
    c. Military status is private, so it cannot be revealed in court documents.
    d. For various reasons, some documents are sealed, so they are not accessible to the public.

2. Based on the preceding passage, which of the following statements is most accurate?
    a. Each state determines how and when court records can be accessed by the public.
    b. A judge should seal all court records for minors.
    c. A judge can seal a court record for any reason.
    d. California allows all court records to be accessed by county record databases.

Questions 3 and 4 are based on the following passage:

Conducting a traffic stop can be one of the most dangerous parts of being a police officer. In light of the many traffic stop incidents that have occurred all over the country, many states are looking at how to address the problem. Recently, the state of Illinois passed a new law that adds traffic stop training to their driver's education courses. These courses are aimed to make new drivers prepared for all the possibilities of the road, and a potential traffic stop by a police officer is one of those possibilities. Proponents of traffic stop training say that this could help new drivers, especially young teens, not to panic in the event they get pulled over. If they know what to expect and how to handle a traffic stop, it is hoped that they could protect themselves from doing anything that could be perceived as a threat, such as reaching under the seat or arguing with the officer. As this new driver's education component gains popularity, it could be seen in more states across the US, and hopefully reduce the amount of traffic stop incidents.

3. Based on the preceding passage, which of the following statements is most accurate?
    a. A new law in Illinois makes it required for all drivers to take driver's education courses.
    b. Lawmakers believe that traffic stop training will help police officers stop more underage drivers.
    c. Arguing with an officer is illegal during a traffic stop.
    d. The new law in Illinois adds traffic stop training to driver's education courses.

4. Based on the preceding passage, which of the following statements is most accurate?
    a. Traffic stops are not dangerous.
    b. Police officers can teach new drivers how to act when they are pulled over.
    c. Traffic stop training aims to protect young drivers from panicking when they are pulled over.
    d. Young drivers should not worry about being pulled over if they are driving safely.

Questions 5 and 6 are based on the following passage:

> Federal law does not restrict the open carry of a weapon in public. Each state determines its own open carry laws. While there are some restrictions to these laws, such as having to gain a permit, or the prohibition of carrying a weapon in certain locations, such as a school or on public transportation, most states allow the open carry of a handgun. Currently, thirty-one states allow private citizens to open carry a firearm without a license. Only three states, California, Florida, and Illinois, and the District of Columbia, prohibit open carry of a firearm. Concealed carry refers to carrying a firearm under clothing or in a way that is not visible to the casual observer. Every state and the District of Columbia allow the concealed carry of a firearm in some form. Forty-two states do require a permit for concealed carry. Of these forty-two states, some have a "may issue" law that allows for wider denial of the permit and others have a "shall issue" law, which generally accepts most permits without discretion.

5. Based on the preceding passage, which of the following statements is most accurate?
    a. Open carry laws are strict in all fifty states.
    b. Only California, Florida, and Illinois allow for open carry of a firearm without a permit.
    c. Nineteen states require a permit for open carry of a firearm.
    d. Most states allow for open carry of a firearm with limited restrictions.

6. Based on the preceding passage, which of the following statements is most accurate?
    a. Eight states require a permit for concealed carry of a firearm in public.
    b. States that have a "may issue" law have very little restrictions on who can get a concealed carry permit.
    c. All states allow for the concealed carry of a firearm in public.
    d. States that have a "shall issue" law have strict restrictions on who can carry a weapon.

Questions 7 and 8 are based on the following passage:

> Since the 1966 Supreme Court case, Miranda v. Arizona, police officers have been required to read the Miranda rights, or Miranda warning, to any person taken into police custody. The Miranda rights include the following:
>
> 1. You have the right to remain silent.
> 2. Anything you say can and will be used against you in a court of law.
> 3. You have the right to an attorney.
> 4. If you cannot afford an attorney, one will be appointed for you.

To fully comply with Miranda rights, the person in custody must also waive their rights, typically in writing. If they do not waive their rights, any information they provide is not admissible in court. Police officers are required to read these rights so that the person in custody is aware of them, but also to protect the information that is given in any questioning they might conduct. When a person in custody is not Mirandized, anything they say, such as a confession, or the location of evidence, cannot be used in court.

7. Based on the preceding passage, which of the following statements is most accurate?
   a. The Miranda rights require the person in custody to remain silent.
   b. The Miranda rights are the result of a Supreme Court case.
   c. Police officers are not always required to read the Miranda rights to a person in custody.
   d. The Miranda rights tell the person in custody that they don't need a lawyer.

8. Based on the preceding passage, which of the following statements is most accurate?
   a. Miranda rights only protect the person in custody.
   b. Police officers who do not read Miranda rights to a person in custody can be sued.
   c. A person must waive their Miranda rights in order for the information they provide to be admissible in court.
   d. Any information gained from a person in custody who has not waived their Miranda rights can be used in court.

Questions 9 and 10 are based on the following passage:

Many police departments have begun using social media outlets such as Twitter, Facebook, and Instagram to their benefit. Police departments have found that the use of social media can be very helpful in identifying suspects, alerting the community to a possible threat, locating a missing person, and even gaining support for their organization. Social media is a two-way street, so police departments are also able to get valuable information and feedback from the communities they serve. Departments who use social media report that when their community feels like they have a forum to voice their opinion, it creates a sense of trust in the police. Departments that do opt to use social media should abide by some simple rules such as limiting the amount of information released, especially on ongoing cases, using appropriate language, and having a single point of contact to manage the sites for continuity. Social media can be a great asset to any police department if used appropriately.

9. Based on the preceding passage, which of the following statements is most accurate?
   a. Police departments should make a Facebook page, but avoid Twitter and Instagram.
   b. Social media has been helpful to police departments in identifying suspects and locating missing persons.
   c. Community trust is not built through the use of social media outlets.
   d. Social media can be helpful to police departments, but it is not used very often.

10. Based on the preceding passage, which of the following statements is most accurate?
    a. Police departments should try to use a single person to manage social media pages.
    b. Police departments should make full use of social media by revealing the details of ongoing cases.
    c. Social media is not beneficial in ongoing cases.
    d. Police departments that want to use social media should hire a consultant to set up their sites.

Questions 11 and 12 are based on the following passage:

A Drug Free School Zone indicates an area where drug offenses carry stricter penalties. This policy was created in the 1970s to deter citizens from committing drug crimes on or around school grounds. A Drug Free School Zone is part of federal law, but states can vary the penalties enforced on those who are convicted of drug-related violations near school campuses. What constitutes a Drug Free School Zone is determined by each jurisdiction, but typically includes school grounds, adjacent areas within 1000 feet, and school buses. Since the 1970s, all fifty states and Washington D.C. have adopted a Drug Free School Zone policy. More recently, some states have reduced the penalties, believing them to be too harsh for minor drug offenses that happened to occur near a school.

11. Based on the previous passage, which of the following statements best describes the purpose of a Drug Free School Zone?
    a. To help police locate and arrest students who are dealing drugs.
    b. To help school staff to locate and eliminate the use of drugs on campus.
    c. To deter people from committing drug-related crimes on and around schools.
    d. To eliminate the use of drugs on school buses.

12. Based on the previous passage, which of the following statements is most accurate?
    a. All fifty states have a 1000-foot zone around each school building that is designated as a Drug Free School Zone.
    b. The Drug Free School Zone enforces stricter penalties on those committed of drug-related offenses on or around school grounds.
    c. The Drug Free School Zone does not include school buses.
    d. Most states have abandoned the Drug Free School Zone policy because the penalties are too harsh.

Questions 13 and 14 are based on the following passage:

Any division of government (federal, state, local) can declare a state of emergency. A state of emergency means that the government has suspended the normal constitutional procedures. In this case, citizens may not have the same rights that they typically do, such as driving on public roadways or whether they can remain in their homes. A state of emergency is typically declared in the wake of a disaster. Disasters can include hurricanes, tornadoes, floods, snowstorms, wildfires, and issues of public health such as a flu outbreak. In the event of a major snowstorm, for example, a government can issue a state of emergency to clear roads for emergency responders and to keep citizens safely in their homes. Declaring a state of emergency can also allow a government to access the use of funds, personnel, equipment, and supplies that are reserved for such a situation.

13. Based on the previous passage, which of the following statements best describes a state of emergency?
    a. The government suspends normal constitutional operations.
    b. Curfews are imposed by the government.
    c. All citizens must remain in their homes.
    d. The government can remove all citizens' rights

14. Which of the following statements is most accurate based on the preceding passage?
    a. Declaring a state of emergency guarantees states will receive federal funding.
    b. Only state government can declare a state of emergency.
    c. Declaring a state of emergency allows the government to access reserved funding, personnel, and supplies.
    d. A state of emergency does not include issues of public health.

Questions 15 and 16 are based on the following passage:

> In the event of a riot, police officers need to be prepared with the necessary gear to manage a large and potentially dangerous crowd. Front line riot police officers are equipped with helmets, riot shields, and body armor for protection. They also may carry gas masks in the event that tear gas is used to incapacitate or disperse a crowd. Riot police officers do have firearms, but less lethal methods of crowd management are preferred. Officers have traditionally used batons and whips to manage unruly crowds. In more recent years, police have begun using more effective methods such as tear gas, pepper spray, tasers, and rubber bullets.

15. The main idea of this passage is best stated with which of the following sentences?
    a. Riot police use gas masks for protection from tear gas and pepper spray.
    b. Violent crowds should always be incapacitated with tear gas.
    c. Batons and whips are not very good methods of crowd control.
    d. Riot police must be prepared with the necessary equipment to manage a dangerous crowd.

16. Which of the following statements is most accurate based on the preceding passage?
    a. Body armor, helmets, and riot shields are used to protect officers in the front line of a riot.
    b. Unruly crowds don't usually require tear gas or pepper spray.
    c. Police are free to use lethal methods to control a dangerous crowd.
    d. Rubber bullets are much less dangerous than regular bullets.

Questions 17 and 18 are based on the following passage:

> K-9 officers are specially trained police officers that handle police dogs. Officers are typically required to have three to five years of patrol experience before applying to a K-9 position. In addition to their traditional training, K-9 officers are required to complete several weeks of official K-9 training to be certified. This training includes skills such as drug and explosive detection, dog handling, crowd control, and search and rescue techniques. Most police dogs live and work with their handlers, so a K-9 officer will be expected to care for his or her dog full time. Most police dogs have ten-year careers, so this is a long-term commitment between dog and officer.

17. Which of the following statements best identifies the main idea of the preceding passage?
    a. Police dogs live and work with their handlers.
    b. K-9 officers should be prepared for a long-term commitment when they apply for this position.
    c. There are several requirements to becoming a K-9 officer.
    d. Patrol experience is necessary to apply for a K-9 officer position.

18. Which of the following statements is most accurate, based on the preceding passage?
    a. K-9 training involves learning search and rescue techniques.
    b. Crowd control is not part of K-9 training.
    c. K-9 training can take up to ten years.
    d. Three to five years of dog training experience are required to become a K-9 officer.

Questions 19 and 20 are based on the following passage:

The Americans with Disabilities Act (ADA) was passed in 1990 to prohibit discrimination and to grant equal opportunity to those with disabilities in employment, transportation, communication, education, government services, and access to public places. In 2008, the ADA was amended to include a broader definition of the term "disability." Those who have physical or mental impairments that limit their lives in one or more major aspects can be considered disabled. This includes, but is not limited to, vision, speech, and hearing impairments, paralysis, intellectual disabilities such as mental retardation, mental illness, and chronic conditions such as epilepsy or multiple sclerosis. Temporary or naturally occurring conditions such as a broken limb, pregnancy, or the flu are not considered disabilities under this act.

19. Which of the following statements best defines the term *disability*?
    a. A physical or mental impairment that limits a major aspect of life.
    b. Vision, speech, and hearing impairments that prevent a person from working.
    c. Any illness that prevents a person from completing their daily tasks, such as the flu.
    d. Mental illnesses such as depression, anxiety, schizophrenia, and bipolar disorder.

20. Based on the passage, which of the following statements is most accurate?
    a. The ADA prevents discrimination, but does not protect equal opportunity for the disabled.
    b. Chronic conditions such as diabetes can be considered a disability if they affect at least one major aspect of a person's life.
    c. Those with a broken limb can apply for temporary handicapped tags.
    d. In 2008 the ADA made changes to what constitutes a major aspect of life.

Answer Explanations

1. D: Based on the passage, the most accurate statement is that some court records are sealed for reasons such as protecting the privacy of a minor involved in the case. While many court records can be accessed in online databases, some must be requested from a specific department such as the Appellate Court. The majority of court records are considered part of the public domain, but not all records are made public. Military status is part of court documents and can therefore be revealed through those records that are made part of the public domain.

2. A: Based on the passage, the most accurate statement is that each state makes its own laws about how and when court records can be accessed by the public. While a judge can seal a record for a minor, it is not required. Also, judges do have the power to seal a record, but this is usually only done in extraordinary circumstances. In California, only some court records are available through county databases. Appellate and Supreme Court records must be accessed through the Appellate Court.

3. D: Based on the passage, the new law discussed will add training in what to do at a traffic stop to driver's education courses in Illinois, so this is the best answer. The new law only adds this component to the courses; it does not require that all drivers take the course. The law does not target underage drivers, but aims to protect them from doing anything risky during a stop, so the goal is not to pull over more teens. While it is not advised that drivers reach under the seat or argue with the officer, it is not illegal. Drivers should know their rights and exercise them.

4. C: Based on the passage, the best answer is that traffic stop training is aimed to prevent drivers from panicking when they are pulled over. Traffic stops are actually one of the more dangerous parts of being a police officer. While a young driver may learn from a police officer during a traffic stop, the paragraph focuses more on how driver's education courses are being updated to instruct young drivers on how to handle a traffic stop. The paragraph is stressing a need for education in what to do during a traffic stop, so the last statement contradicts that point. A driver who believes he is driving safely could still be stopped.

5. D: This statement is the most accurate because the passage states that thirty-one states allow private citizens to open carry a firearm without a license. Thus, open carry laws are not very strict in all fifty states. California, Florida, and Illinois are singled out not because they allow open carry without a permit, but because they are the only states that prohibit open carry of a firearm. Because of these states' laws on open carry, the final statement about nineteen states requiring a permit cannot be true.

6. C: This is the most accurate statement because the passage asserts that all states including the District of Columbia allow for concealed carry of a firearm in public. The passage states that forty-two states, not eight, require a permit for concealed carry of a firearm in public. The "may issue" law allows states to pose more restrictions on who can be granted a concealed carry permit, while the "shall issue" law is much less restrictive.

7. B: The passage begins by stating the Miranda rights have been required since the 1966 Supreme Court case of Miranda v. Arizona, so this is the most accurate statement. The Miranda rights do not require the person in custody to remain silent, but notify them that they may remain silent if they choose to. Police officers must read the Miranda rights to any person in custody to protect the information they may get in interrogation. The Miranda rights tell the person in custody that they have the right to an attorney and that one will be provided to them if they cannot afford an attorney.

8. C: This statement is the most accurate because the passage states that in order to comply with Miranda rights, a person in custody must waive their rights. Miranda rights protect both the person in custody and the police. They also protect the admissibility of the information gained in any questioning. While police officers could be sued for any number of reasons, the passage does not make any indication that they could be sued for not reading a person in custody their Miranda rights. When a person has not waived their Miranda rights, the information they provide may not be admissible in court.

9. B: The passage indicates that police departments can successfully use social media to identify suspects and find missing persons. The passage does not deter police departments from using any social media outlet. Trust can be built with the community when they feel they have a voice through police social media sites. The passage states that the use of social media by police departments is actually growing in popularity.

10. A: Based on the passage, this statement is the most accurate because it calls for a single point of contact to manage the sites for continuity. The passage actually calls for police departments to limit details on ongoing cases, but it does not say it is not beneficial in these cases. For example, the paragraph states that social media can be helpful in identifying a suspect, which would be for an ongoing case. That does not mean they should reveal all the details of the crime or anything that might jeopardize the case. While some departments may opt to hire a consultant to set up their social media sites, nothing in the paragraph suggests that this is necessary.

11. C: Based on the passage, the best description of the purpose of a Drug Free School Zone is to deter citizens from committing drug related crimes on and around school campuses. Nothing in the passage suggests the law was created to help police identify students who are dealing drugs. The laws do not help schools identify drug use on campus; they only make penalties stricter for those who do. While a Drug Free School Zone may help deter drug use on school buses, this is not the primary purpose of the policy.

12. B: Based on the passage, the most accurate statement is that Drug Free School Zones enforce stricter penalties on those committing drug offenses on or near school grounds. While some states do enforce a 1000-foot zone around schools, the passage states that this is only typically the case, and is not the case for all fifty states. The Drug Free School Zone does include buses in most states. The passage notes that some states have reduced penalties in Drug Free School Zones, deeming them too harsh, but it does not say that most states have abandoned the policy.

13. A: The statement that best defines a state of emergency is the suspension of normal constitutional operation. While a curfew may be imposed when a state of emergency is declared, this is not always the case. Citizens may need to remain in their homes, but in the case of a hurricane or flood, evacuations may be necessary, so this answer is incorrect. While a government does have a right to alter citizens' rights in a state of emergency, it is to maintain their safety, and does not extend to all of their rights as citizens.

14. C: Based on the passage, the best answer is that a state of emergency allows the government access to reserved supplies, funding, and personnel. The passage does not suggest that a state of emergency will guarantee federal funding to any government. Local, state, and federal government can declare a state of emergency. The passage states that issues of public health can be addressed with a state of emergency declaration.

15. D: This statement best captures the main idea, or main point of the paragraph, which is to show the necessary equipment police officers must have to best manage a riot. While riot police do use gas masks for protection, this is too specific to be the main idea of the paragraph. The passage mentions tear gas, but does not suggest it is the best method to manage a crowd, so this is not the main focus of the paragraph. The passage does mention that better methods of crowd control than batons and whips have been used in recent years, but this is a supporting detail, and not the main idea of the passage.

16. A: This is the most accurate statement based on the passage, because it directly states that front line riot police use these methods of protection. The passage does not determine whether crowds typically require tear gas or pepper spray. The passage states that less lethal methods are preferred over lethal methods. While rubber bullets are less dangerous than regular bullets, this is not mentioned in the passage.

17. C: This answer best identifies the main idea of the passage, which is to detail the requirements of becoming a K-9 officer. Police dogs do typically live and work with their handlers, and this is a long-term commitment, but these answers represent supporting details of the passage, not the main idea. Patrol experience is typically a requirement of becoming a K-9 officer, but again this is a supporting detail, not the main idea of the passage.

18. A: This statement is the most accurate because the passage lists search and rescue techniques as one of the skills learned in K-9 officer training. According to the passage, crowd control is a skill learned in K-9 training. K-9 training takes several weeks, not ten years. K-9 officers are required to have three to five years of patrol experience, not dog training experience, based on the passage.

19. A: Based on the passage, this statement best defines the term *disability*, which is a physical or mental impairment that limits a person in at least one major aspect of life. While visual, speech, and hearing impairments can be considered disabilities, they are examples of a disability and not a comprehensive definition. Illnesses such as the flu are temporary and cannot be considered a disability, nor is this a definition for the term *disability*. While these mental illnesses may be considered disabilities, again they are examples, and not a comprehensive definition of the term *disability*.

20. B: This statement is most accurate because the passage states that chronic conditions can be considered a disability as long as they affect one major aspect of a person's life. The ADA prevents discrimination and also protects equal opportunity for the disabled. While it may be true that a person with a broken limb can apply for a temporary handicapped tag, the paragraph doesn't mention this, so it is not the most accurate statement based on the passage. The ADA was amended in 2008 to make a broader description of the term *disability*, not to change what constitutes a major aspect of life.

Cloze Test

The California POST will assess reading comprehension skills through a Cloze Test, an exercise that measures how well readers understand what they've read as they read it. Test-takers will be given a passage of text from which words have been deleted and replaced with blanks.

The passage will have forty blanks in total, and the goal is to determine the missing words (fill in the blanks) by using the given context clues. Context clues are hints that the author gives to help readers understand the overall meaning of the text. The first and the last sentences of the passage will be complete.

On the exam, there will not be a list of words to choose from—this section is not multiple-choice. The number of letters in each missing word will be given. Each blank space will be composed of dashes; each dash represents one letter of the missing word. For example, if there are four dashes, then the word is four letters long: _ _ _ _.

The word selected will be considered correct only if it is correct in terms of both grammar and meaning. For example, it has to be the *right part of speech* (a verb, a noun, an adjective), and it has to *fit into the sentence* in the right way (plural/singular, past/present).

For some blanks, there will be more than one potential right answer. For others, though, only one word will be the right fit. If more than one word is a potential correct answer, then credit be will received as long as the above criteria are met.

To prepare for the Cloze Test, it's helpful to review the parts of speech to see how they collectively function to form complete sentences (sentences with a subject and a predicate, also called *independent clauses*). Familiarity with parts of speech strengthens one's ability to fill in the blanks of the Cloze exercise correctly.

The Eight Parts of Speech		
Nouns	refer to people, places, things, or ideas	*mother, school, book, beauty*
Pronouns	alternatives for nouns	*I, you, she, it, this*
Verbs	express action or states of being	*run, drive, appear, remember*
Adjectives	modify nouns	*dark blue, average*
Adverbs	modify verbs; answer *when? where? how?* and *why?*	*soon, there, happily, entirely*
Prepositions	express the relationship between a noun and another element	*about, before, through, after*
Coordinating conjunctions	used to connect clauses or sentences or to coordinate words in the same clause	*and, but, for, yet, nor, so*
Interjections	exclamations	*Wow! Hi!*

Nouns

A *noun* is a word used to describe a person, place, thing, or idea. They are often the subject, object, or direct object of a sentence. There are five main types of nouns:

- Common nouns
- Proper nouns
- General nouns
- Specific nouns
- Collective nouns

Common nouns are general words that can be used to name people, places, and things:

- People: mom, brother, neighbor
- Places: office, gym, restaurant
- Things: bed, computer, sandwich

Proper nouns are specific words that can be used to name people, places, and things. For example:

- People: Amelia Earhart, Albert Einstein, Stephen Hawking
- Places: Philadelphia, Pennsylvania; Bombay, India; Australia
- Brands: Levi's jeans, Apple computer

Note the difference between common and proper nouns:

- Common noun: The suspect said that she'd eaten breakfast with her sister that morning.
- Proper noun: The suspect said that she'd eaten breakfast with Jane Lowe that morning.

Sometimes common and proper nouns appear in the same sentence:

George Washington was the first *president*.

General nouns are words used to describe conditions or ideas. They are abstract by nature. For example:

- Condition: bravery, love
- Idea: justice, freedom

Specific nouns are words used to describe particular people, places, and things. For example:

- People: victim, perpetrator, officer
- Places: city, beach, stadium
- Things: holster, badge, custody

Collective nouns are words used to refer to groups of people, places, or things as a whole. For example, *flock, group, bunch, crowd, tribe,* and *pack* are all collective nouns.

Pronouns

A *pronoun* is a word that replaces a noun in a sentence. There are seven types:

- Personal
- Reflexive
- Relative
- Interrogative
- Demonstrative
- Indefinite
- Reciprocal

Personal Pronouns

Personal pronouns are words that represent specific people or things (for example, I, you, he, she, me, you, and mine).

Three things must be considered in choosing the correct personal pronoun: *grammatical case*, *quantity*, and *point of view*.

Grammatical Case

A noun or pronoun's case refers to its relationship to the other words in a sentence. There are three cases of pronouns:

Nominative	nouns and pronouns that are the subject of a verb	I, we, you, he, she, it, they
Objective	nouns and pronouns that are the direct or indirect objects of a verb	Me, us, you, him, her, it, they
Possessive	used to show ownership	Me, mine, ours, your, yours, his, her, hers, its, their

Quantity

When referring to a quantity that is more than, the pronouns must be singular (I, him, you—one person). When referring to a quantity of more than one, the pronoun must be plural (we, their, your—several people).

Point of View

Point of view refers to perspective. There are three types of point of view:

First person refers to the perspective of the person speaking.

> *I* did not do anything.

Second person refers to the perspective of a person being spoken to.

> *You* are a witness.

Third person refers to the perspective of a person being spoken about.

> *The suspect* fled the vicinity.

Reflexive Pronouns

Reflexive pronouns are preceded by the adverb, adjective, pronoun, or noun to which they refer. They are used to rename the subjects of action verbs or function as different types of objects: *myself, himself, herself, themselves, yourself, yourselves, ourselves.*

> She was in a hurry, so she did the reports *herself*.

Intensive pronouns are reflexive pronouns that are only used to add *emphasis* to the subject of a sentence; they aren't required for meaning: *myself, yourself, himself, herself, itself, ourselves, yourselves,* and *themselves.*

> We met the king *himself*.

Relative Pronouns

Relative pronouns are used to connect phrases or clauses to a noun or pronoun. There are eight relative pronouns: *that, which, who, whom, whose, whichever, whoever,* and *whomever*.

> The first point of entry was closed, *which* meant we had to enter through the back.

Interrogative Pronouns

Interrogative pronouns are used to ask a question. There are five interrogative pronouns: *what, which, who, whom,* and *whose*.

> *Whose* boots are those?

Special note about *who/whom*: substitute *he* for *who* and *him* for *whom* to determine which should be used.

> [*Who* or *whom*] wrote that email?

> He wrote that email?

> Him wrote that email?

He=who, so *who* is correct.

> She gave the presentation to [*who* or *whom*]?

> She gave the presentation to he?

> She gave the presentation to him?

Him=whom, so *whom* is correct.

Demonstrative Pronouns

Demonstrative pronouns take the place of a noun phrase. There are six demonstrative pronouns: *this, that, these, those, none,* and *neither.*

> *That* is not the right thing to do.

Indefinite pronouns are used when referring to a person or thing in a general way. Some examples *include all, another, any, anyone, each, everything, nobody, and several.*

> *Each* is separated by category.

Reciprocal Pronouns

Reciprocal pronouns are used when two or more people have done something simultaneously. The two reciprocal pronouns are: *each other* and *one another.*

> They were kind to *each other.*

Verbs

Verbs are words that express actions or occurrences; they signal the sentence's predicate (what the subject is doing). While a noun is often the subject of a sentence, the verb expresses what is happening or what has happened. For a sentence to be complete, a verb must be included. There are three main types of verbs: *action, linking,* and *helping.*

Action Verbs

Action verbs are verbs that show that something is happening, or that something/someone is in possession of something else.

> Security personnel *detained* the prisoner.

> Detective Suarez *has* a subject in custody.

There are two types of action verbs: transitive and intransitive.

Transitive verbs refer to an object that is receiving the action. There must be a direct object.

> The sergeant apprehended the suspect.

The transitive verb in this sentence is *apprehended. The suspect* is the verb's direct object, that is, that which receives the action. Without the direct object to go along with the transitive verb, the sentence wouldn't make sense: *the sergeant apprehended.* Transitive verbs can be active or passive:

A verb is *active* if the subject of the sentence performs the action. Transitive active verbs are the verbs in sentences with direct objects.

> Officer Lee *pursued* the suspect.

The subject, *Officer Lee*, performed the action, *pursued*, and *the suspect* is the direct object that receives that action.

The verb is *passive* if the subject or direct object is on the receiving end of the action.

> The suspect *was pursued* by Officer Lee.

In this sentence, the subject of the sentence is *the suspect* and it is receiving Officer Lee's action.

Intransitive verbs are action words that don't need direct objects.

The recruits progressed well.

The verb in this sentence is *progressed*. We know it is an intransitive verb because a direct object (what they progressed in or with) is unnecessary for the sentence to be complete.

Linking Verbs

Linking verbs are verbs that link the subject of the sentence to more information about that subject.

The altercation *was* verbal.

In this sentence, *the altercation* is the subject, and we learn something new about it—*what kind* of altercation it was. *Was* serves as the verb in this sentence, linking the subject and the added information.

Common Linking Verbs			
is	are	seems	feels
was	become	might	am

Some action verbs can also be linking verbs.

The defendant *appeared* before the court.

In the sentence above, *appeared* is an action verb.

The defendant *appeared remorseful* when addressing the judge.

In the sentence above, *appeared* links the defendant to the subject complement, *remorseful.*

Helping Verbs

Helping verbs are words that appear before action or linking verbs. Their purpose is to add information about either time or possibility. The addition of a helping verb to an action or linking verb creates a verb phrase.

Andrew *is appearing* before the judge.

In this sentence, *Andrew* is the subject, *is* is the helping verb, and *appearing* is the action verb.

Common Helping Verbs			
am	is	are	was
were	be	being	been
have	has	had	do
does	did	done	could
should	would	can	might

Conjugation

Conjugation refers to changing verbs to indicate *point of view, number, tense,* and *mood.* It also refers to subject/verb agreement.

Point of View
Verbs are conjugated to match the point of view of the subject of a sentence.

> I *am* a police officer.

In this sentence, *am* is a conjugation of the verb *to be*, for the subject *I*. *I to be a police officer*, or *I are a police officer*, are incorrect.

Number
Verbs are conjugated to indicate how many people are involved in the action of a sentence.

> *She runs* a ten-minute mile.

> *They run* every day.

The verb *to run* is conjugated by adding an *s* to indicate that one person is running. If the action includes more than one person, the conjugation changes: an *s* is not needed.

Tense
The tense of a verb indicates when the action is taking place. There are six possible verb tenses:

- Present: The action is currently happening or happens habitually.
- Past: The action has happened already.
- Future: The action will happen at a later date.
- Present perfect: The action started in the past and continues.
- Past perfect: Two actions occurred in the past, one before the other.
- Future perfect: The action will be complete before another action occurs in the future.

Conjugating a verb so that it is in the present or past tense is as simple as changing the form through letter addition or substitution. For the other tenses, including future, present perfect, past perfect, and future perfect, a helping verb is required.

Present: I run.	*Present perfect*: I have run.
Past: I ran.	*Past perfect*: I had run.
Future: I will run.	*Future perfect*: I will have run.

Mood
The *mood* indicates the purpose of a sentence and the speaker's general attitude. There are five common moods:

- Indicative: used for facts, opinions, and questions.

  > The officer wrote a ticket. ← This is a statement of fact.

- Imperative: used for orders and requests.

  > Put your hands on the vehicle. ← This is an order.

- Interrogative: used for questioning.

  Will you stand down? ← This is a question.

- Conditional: used in a "what if" conditional state that will cause something else to happen.

  I might break my arm if I slip on the ice. ← This is a "what if" causal scenario.

- Subjunctive: used for wishes and other statements that are doubtful or not factual.

  I wish that no one used drugs. ← This expresses a wish.

<u>Voice</u>
The voice of a verb is active if the subject of the sentence is performing the action. If the subject is on the receiving end of the action, the verb is passive. See also *transitive verbs*.

Adjectives

An *adjective* is a word used to modify or describe a noun or pronoun. By answering questions about the noun or pronoun, adjectives make a sentence more specific. An adjective usually answers one of three questions:

- Which one?

  The *older* brother was seen entering the building.

  In this sentence, the *brother* is the subject. The adjective, *older*, tells us which one.

- What kind?

  Professional officers can become detectives.

  In this sentence, the adjective, *professional,* tells us what kind of officer can become a detective.

- How many or how often?

  She drinks milk *five* times a day.

  In this sentence, the adjective, *five*, tells us how many times a day the person drinks milk.

<u>Articles</u>
Another type of adjective is an *article*, which is used to identify a noun in a sentence. There are three articles in the English language: *the, a,* and *an. The* is a *definite* article, and *a* and *an* are *indefinite* articles, so it's important to choose the right one for meaning.

The is used when there is a limited number (definite) of something being referred to.

  I left *the book* on the couch.

In this sentence, the noun being referred to is *book*. Choosing the article *the* indicates that one particular book was left on the couch.

A and *an* are used when there is not a fixed amount (indefinite) of something being referred to.

I left *a book* on the couch.

Again, the noun in the sentence is *book.* The article changed to *a* because the sentence no longer refers to one specific book.

On the Cloze Test, it will be important to remember that *an* comes before nouns that begin with a vowel.

I left *an old* book on the couch.

<u>Comparisons</u>
Adjectives can also be used to make comparisons. These adjectives come in two forms: relative and absolute.

Relative adjectives show a comparison between two things. There are three degrees of relative adjectives: *positive, comparative*, and *superlative.*

- Positive: the base form of the adjective

    The painting was *beautiful.*

- *Comparative*: a higher level of some quality of the adjective

    The painting was *more* beautiful than I expected it to be.

- *Superlative*: The highest form of quality of the adjective

    The painting was the *most beautiful* painting I've ever seen.

Absolute adjectives also show comparison, but not in varying degrees; they're *non-gradable.* A good example of an absolute adjective is *empty.* If there are two boxes, and one of them is *empty*, the other box cannot be *emptier, more emptier,* or *most empty.* The box is either empty or it is not. *Empty* is an absolute adjective.

Adverbs

An *adverb* is a word or phrase that modifies verbs, adjectives, or other adverbs. Like adjectives, adverbs are also words that can be used to answer questions. Adverbs answer the following:

- When? She drove *yesterday.*
- Where? They drove *here.*
- How? He drove *quickly.*
- To what extent? She drives *whenever possible.*
- Why? We ride the bus *to avoid traffic.*

As seen in the examples, some adverbs end in *–ly*, but not all. The words *not* and *never* are considered adverbs because they modify adjectives.

Again, like adjectives, adverbs can be used to make comparisons in three degrees: *positive, comparative,* and *superlative.*

- They *quietly* went into the building.
- The squad went into the building *more quietly* than the cadets.
- The squad leader went into the building *most quietly.*

Prepositions

A *preposition* is a word that appears in a sentence to show the relationship between a noun or pronoun and another element.

The books are *on* the shelves.

The preposition, *on,* shows the relationship between the books (noun) and the shelves (another noun).

Common Prepositions				
aboard	behind	during	outside	to
about	below	for	over	toward
above	beyond	inside	past	under
among	by	into	since	upon
around	despite	near	through	within

Conjunctions

Conjunctions join pieces of words, phrases, or clauses. There are three types of conjunctions: *coordinating, correlative,* and *subordinating.*

Coordinating Conjunctions
Coordinating conjunctions connect equal parts of sentences. Common coordinating conjunctions are *for, and, nor, but, or, yet, so* (sometimes called the FANBOYS).

The poem was brief, *but* it was beautiful.

In this sentence *but* connects two independent clauses into one sentence.

In some cases, coordinating conjunctions convey a sense of contrast. In the example above, the poem's beauty is in contrast to the length of it.

Correlative Conjunctions
Correlative conjunctions show the connection between pairs. Common correlative conjunctions are *either/or, neither/nor, not only/but also, both/and, whether/or,* and *so/as.*

Either you're having lunch at home, *or* you're eating out.

In this sentence, *either* and *or* are used to connect two options.

<u>Subordinating Conjunctions</u>

Subordinating conjunctions join dependent clauses with independent clauses, providing a transition between two ideas. This transition often adds information about time, place, or the effect of something.

Our team lost the game *because* Jim was unprepared.

In this sentence, *because* is connecting two clauses and indicating a cause and effect relationship between them.

Common Subordinating Conjunctions		
after	since	whenever
although	so that	where
because	unless	wherever
before	when	in order that

Interjections

An *interjection* is an exclamatory word used to indicate extreme emotion or feeling. Some examples include *Hey! Oh!* and *Wow!*

These words can be used alone as a complete sentence, or they can be added to a sentence to indicate a forceful change in thought or add feeling.

Wow! You look great today!

Hey, in my opinion, he deserves the presidency.

In the first sentence, *Wow!* is the interjection used to add feeling to the speaker's opinion. In the second sentence, the speaker uses *Hey* to grab the listener's attention before expressing their opinion.

Practice Questions

Instructions: In the fictional narrative below, wherever you see a dashed blank line, you have to supply the correct word. The dashes equal the number of letters in the missing word. For a word to be considered correct, it must make sense in the passage, and it must have the same number of letters as there are dashes.

There may be a break in the biggest, most perplexing art heist case of the past thirty years. The Federal Bureau of Investigation (FBI) told reporters (1) _ _ _ _ _ that video footage from the time of the robbery has been discovered. In 1985, paintings valued at over $400 million were (2) _ _ _ _ _ _ from the Fine (3) _ _ _ _ Museum. The stolen works were considered to be some of the most important of the museum's collection and included (4) _ _ _ _ _ _ _ _ _ by Rembrandt, Manet, Van Gogh, and Vermeer.

It was Thursday, July 8, 1985 when a man dressed as a teacher entered the museum after hours. (5) _ _ told the museum's two security (6) _ _ _ _ _ _ that he believed a (7) _ _ _ _ _ had been separated from his school group during the museum's closing. The guards, (8) _ _ _ had noticed several (9) _ _ _ _ _ _ groups touring the museum that day, thought it was plausible that a child could have been (10) _ _ _ _ behind. They allowed the (11) _ _ _ _ _ _ _, who was in a panic, to accompany them through the halls of the museum, where they called to the missing (12) _ _ _ _ _ _ _. It was then that the teacher managed to detain the (13) _ _ _ _ _ _ in a closet, binding their hands and feet with duct tape.

The guards managed to free (14) _ _ _ _ _ _ _ _ _ _ in what they estimated after the fact to be (15) _ _ _ _ _ _ _ _ _ _ _ ten minutes. They quickly summoned the police and locked down the museum in accordance with robbery protocols. In just that period of ten (16) _ _ _ _ _ _ _, eight paintings were (17) _ _ _ _ _. At the time of the investigation, this led police and investigators from the FBI's Art Theft Division to estimate that at least three (18) _ _ _ _ _ _ _ must have been involved. This estimation was later called (19) _ _ _ _ question after a journalist suggested that the guards' sense of (20) _ _ _ _ might have been off due to the stress of the situation. If the guards were detained for more than ten minutes, (21) _ _ _ _ _ _ than three thieves could have taken the paintings. Alternatively, if the guards were detained for less than ten minutes, (22) _ _ _ _ than three thieves would have been needed to gain access to the museum.

At the time of the heist, the Chicago Police Department and the FBI both (23) _ _ _ _ _ _ _ that the art would be recovered when the thieves (24) _ _ _ _ _ _ _ _ _ to sell it, as often occurs when very famous works are stolen. Flash-forward more than thirty years, and the art has still (25) _ _ _ to surface. The (26) _ _ _ _ _ _ of time that the thieves have remained at large is not the only unique thing about this case, (27) _ _ _ _ _ _. There have been a number of red herrings, the most notable being the lengthy inquiry into and subsequent arrest of (28) _ _ _ _ _ _ _ men who had installed protective glass in that wing of the museum just a few (29) _ _ _ _ _ prior to the robbery. Though two service men from Anderson Glass were arrested, due to insufficient evidence, namely the paintings (30) _ _ _ _ _ _ _ _ _ _, the U.S. Attorney was unable to (31) _ _ _ _ _ their guilt.

The announcement today that new evidence had been (32) _ _ _ _ _ _ _ _ _ was a shock to many, the FBI included. In a joint statement made by the FBI and the Justice Department, U.S. Attorney Maria Lopez (33) _ _ _ _, "This is the kind of break we always hope for when a case has gone cold." The video footage is not from the museum's security system, but from a convenience store down the street from the museum. The store, Grab'n'Go, has been owned by the same family for forty-five years.

"When my father passed away over the winter, we started to clean out his office at the back of the store," said Casey Initeri, the current (34) _ _ _ _ _ and operator of the store.

"What we found were stacks of old VHS tapes from the store's (35) _ _ _ _ _ _ _ _ camera. My father had a big box of them and would record over old tapes whenever he needed to. (36) _ just saw an article in the paper about the 30th anniversary of the (37) _ _ _ _ _, so the date was on my mind when I saw that the label on one of Dad's tapes read July, 1985. I couldn't believe it. I called the FBI right away."

The FBI has not yet disclosed to the press the (38) _ _ _ _ _ _ _ _ of the tape, so how it will advance the case is still unknown. The thieves (39) _ _ _ _ _ _ approached or retreated from the museum past the convenience store, so it is likely that their vehicle (and maybe even their faces) are on the tape.

Empty frames currently (40) _ _ _ _ on the walls of the Chicago Fine Arts Museum in an eerie testament to the works that were taken. That wing of the museum has become a place not to learn about art, but to speculate about a perfect crime.

Answer Explanations

1. today

2. stolen

3. Arts

4. paintings

5. He

6. guards

7. child

8. who

9. school

10. left

11. teacher

12. student

13. guards

14. themselves

15. approximately

16. minutes

17. taken

18. thieves

19. into

20. time

21. fewer

22. more

23. assumed

24. attempted

25. yet

26. amount

27. though

28. service

29. weeks

30. themselves

31. prove

32. uncovered

33. said

34. owner

35. security

36. I

37. heist/crime

38. contents

39. either

40. hang

Reasoning

Law enforcement officers use their powers of observation to gather information. Through their reasoning skill-sets, they'll make inferences and draw conclusions about information and evidence.

Very broadly, reasoning is an approach to thinking that prioritizes logic. Law enforcement officers use reasoning every day when forming judgments about suspects, piecing together timelines, and evaluating crime scenes.

There are three types of reasoning problems on the California POST:

- Comparative Values
- Numerical Series
- Similar Words

There will be sixteen total Reasoning items on the exam. These items require searches for patterns, similarities, and relationships in order to choose the correct answer. There will be lists of statements, numbers, or words, and test takers will analyze the given information in order to answer the question.

Comparative Values

A *comparative value* item provides details about specific subjects, like types of fruit or family members, and then asks that comparisons be drawn between them. There are two possible tasks:

- Order the subjects from *least to greatest* or *greatest to least*
- Find *the value* of a certain subject

When encountering a comparative value item, it's helpful to make a list and fill it in according to information given in the prompt. Everything needed to answer this type of question correctly is in the question. Here's an example:

> A vehicle rental company stocks cars, vans, busses, and trucks. The company ranks their vehicles by popularity so that they know what to buy when expanding their business. Cars are ranked between vans and trucks. Trucks are more popular than vans. Buses are ranked lowest. Which type of vehicle is rented the most?
>
> a. Cars
> b. Vans
> c. Busses
> d. Trucks

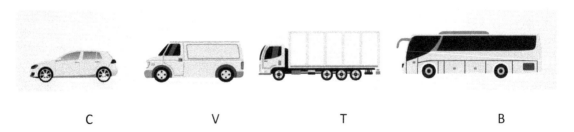

C   V   T   B

The items being compared are the prompt's subjects. In this question, there are cars, vans, buses, and trucks. Assigning them a letter or an image, as illustrated above, is a helpful way to list them quickly. For this question, the first letter of each vehicle represents the subject: C (car), V (van), T (truck), and B (bus).

Note what the prompt actually asks. In this prompt, the goal is to find which vehicle is rented *the most*. Thus the list needs to be ordered from *most to least*:

Vehicles Rented – Most to Least

Determine which information is stated outright, meaning it is known for sure. In this prompt, *buses are ranked the lowest,* so buses can be placed at the bottom of the list:

Vehicles Rented – Most to Least
B

Next, look through the prompt for more information. This prompt states that *cars are ranked between vans and trucks,* so the list can look one of two ways:

Vehicles Rented – Most to Least Possibility 1	Vehicles Rented – Most to Least Possibility 2
V	T
C	C
T	V
B	B

To decide which list is correct, look for the last piece of information given in the prompt. In this prompt, *trucks are more popular than vans.* Which one of the lists shows that to be true?

Vehicles Rented – Most to Least
T
C
V
B

Revisit the final question to determine the response. *Which vehicle is being rented the most?* The answer is *D,* Trucks.

Numerical Series

A *numerical series* item presents a list of numbers and asks test takers to determine what the next number should be. The key to answering this type of question correctly is to understand *the relationship between the numbers* in the series. Do they increase or decrease, and at what rate? Is there a pattern? Here's an example:

> Identify the next number in the series: 7, 14, 21, 28, 35, …
> a. 42
> b. 28
> c. 47
> d. 50

First, decide if the numbers in the list are *increasing* or *decreasing.* Generally, if numbers increase, it is indicative of addition or multiplication. If they decrease, subtraction or division is more likely.

The numbers in this list are *increasing*: 7, 14, 21, 28, 35.

Here's a strategy to determine *the rate* at which they are increasing:

7,　14,　21,　28,　35

+7　+7　+7　+7

The numbers in the list are increasing by 7. The rate of increase is constant throughout the list. Note that not all lists will increase or decrease at a constant rate.

To find the answer to this question, simply continue the rate of increase by adding 7 to 35. The answer is *A*, 42.

Here's a more complicated example:

> Identify the next number in the series: 2, 3, 5, 9, 17…
> a. 24
> b. 33
> c. 37
> d. 39

Again, the first thing to do is decide if the numbers in the list are increasing or decreasing. The numbers in this list are *increasing*: 2, 3, 5, 9, 17.

Next, figure out the rate of increase:

2,　3,　5,　9,　17

+1　+2　+4　+8

Notice that, in this question, the rate of increase is not constant. The question needs to be solved by looking for a pattern in the rate of increase.

2,   3,   5,   9,   17

+1   +2   +4   +8

x2   x2   x2

1, 2, 4, and 8 are all *multiples of 2*: 1 x 2 = 2, 2 x 2 = 4, 4 x 2 = 8. What is needed to continue this pattern? *8 x 2.*

Given that 8 x 2 = 16, 16 is the next number in the rate of increase.

2,   3,   5,   9,   17

+1   +2   +4   +8   +16

x2   x2   x2   x2

So, 16 must be added to the last number in the list to find the answer: 17 + 16 = 33. The answer is *B*, 33.

Similar Words

In *similar words* questions, there will be a set of four words. Three of the words will be similar, and one will be different. The goal is to choose the one word that is *unlike* the other three.

The key to answering these questions correctly is to e*stablish the relationship between the three similar words.* The word that does not share that relationship with the others will be the answer. Here's an example:

Three of the following words are similar, while one is different. Select the word that is different.
a. Pants
b. Closet
c. Dresses
d. Skirts

First, consider what the *theme* of the words is. The theme of this list seems to be *clothing.* Next, start with choice *A* and consider how this word relates to choice *B.* Pants can *be kept* in a closet.

In choices *C* and *D*, dresses and skirts, like pants, can also be kept in a closet. So, three out of four of the words are articles of clothing that can be kept in a closet, rendering *closet* the word that is unlike the others. The answer is *B*, Closet.

Here's another example:

Three of the following words are similar, while one is different. Select the word that is different.

   a. Book
   b. Magazine
   c. Newspaper
   d. Reading

In this question, the theme is *reading*, which is also one of the answer choices. Choices *A*, *B*, and *C* are things that can be read. Though choice *D*, reading, does relate to the other answer choices, it does not relate in the same way. Reading is a verb, not an object that can be read, so the word that does not belong is D, Reading.

Practice Questions

Directions: Officers often face situations in which they need to determine how different pieces of information relate to one another. In this section, you will be presented with information, such as a group or ordered series of facts, numbers, letters, or words. Your task is to study the various pieces of information and try to understand how they relate to one another. Mark the letter that identifies your choice on your answer sheet.

1. Three of the following words are similar, while one is different. Which one is different?
    a. Student
    b. Teacher
    c. Desk
    d. Principal

2. The families who live on Gardenia Drive keep dogs, cats, and rabbits as pets. There are 3 more cats than dogs. There are 5 more dogs than rabbits. There are 2 rabbits. How many cats live on Gardenia Drive?
    a. 10
    b. 4
    c. 2
    d. 11

3. Which of the following is the next number in the series: 2, 13, 4, 14, 8, 15...?
    a. 16
    b. 17
    c. 32
    d. 14

4. A local librarian conducts a poll to gauge what types of baked goods should be sold at the library fundraiser. Cookies are ranked between cakes and pies. Pies are ranked higher than cakes. Cream puffs receive the least number of votes. Which type of baked goods receives the most votes?
    a. Cookies
    b. Cakes
    c. Pies
    d. Cream puffs

5. Three of the following words are similar, while one is different. Which one is different?
    a. Roof
    b. Skylight
    c. Ceiling
    d. Floor

6. Which of the following is the next number in the series: 84, 80, 76, 72, 68...?
    a. 75
    b. 67
    c. 64
    d. 70

7. Which of the following is the next number in the series: 17, 18, 20, 23, 27...?
   a. 29
   b. 33
   c. 23
   d. 32

8. After school, Andrew, Matt and Geeta spend time watching television. Andrew watches more television than Geeta, but less than Matt. Which of the following lists from most to least the friends in order of how much television they watch after school?
   a. Andrew, Matt, Geeta
   b. Not enough information
   c. Geeta, Andrew, Matt
   d. Matt, Andrew, Geeta

9. Three of the following words are similar, while one is different. Which one is different?
   a. Notebook
   b. Pencil
   c. Pen
   d. Crayon

10. Which of the following is the next number in the series: 41, 30, 42, 29, 43, 28...?
    a. 30
    b. 44
    c. 43
    d. 41

11. Alejandro, Jennifer and Walt are competing in their track team's 500-meter dash. Jennifer finished behind Walt but ahead of Alejandro. Who won the race?
    a. Alejandro
    b. Jennifer
    c. Walt
    d. Not enough information

12. Which of the following is the next number in the series: 144, 133, 130, 119, 116...?
    a. 113
    b. 105
    c. 127
    d. 98

13. Three of the following words are similar, while one is different. Which one is different?
    a. Lake
    b. Ocean
    c. River
    d. Boat

14. Which of the following is the next number in the series: 288, 144, 72, 36, 18...?
    a. 4
    b. 12
    c. 6
    d. 9

15. On their driving test, Anna earned 97 points, 12 points more than Michael. Michael scored 10 points higher than Tom, who scored 6 points lower than Jaime. What was Tom's score?

    a. 109

    b. 22

    c. 75

    d. 91

16. Which of the following is the next number in the series: 3, 9, 27, 81, 243...?

    a. 486

    b. 729

    c. 121

    d. 356

Answer Explanations

1. C: The word *desk* is not like the other three. A student, teacher, and principal are all people who are found in a school setting. A desk is an inanimate object that can be found in a school setting, rendering it different from the other three words.

2. A: The correct answer is 10. According to the prompt, there are 2 rabbits on Gardenia Drive. If there are 5 more dogs than rabbits, then there are 7 dogs. If there are 3 more cats than dogs, then 10 cats live on Gardenia Drive.

3. A: The next number in the series is 16. In this series, two patterns of increase can be found. Every other number either doubles or increases by one. So, to find the next number in the series, decide which pattern the missing number should continue. Because 2x2 is 4 and 4x2 is 8, the missing number is 16.

4. C: The correct answer is pies. According to the prompt, cookies are ranked between cakes and pies, and pies are ranked higher than cakes. At this point, the list should read *pies, cookies,* and *cakes.* The last information in the prompt is that cream puffs received the least number of votes, so *pies* remains at the top of the list, having the most votes received.

5. D: The word *floor* is not like the other three. A roof, skylight, and ceiling are all elements of a house or building positioned *above.* The floor is positioned *below,* making it unlike the other three words.

6. C: The next number in the series is 64. In this series, each successive number is 4 less than the number that preceded it. So, to find the next number in the series, subtract 4 from the previous number.

7. D: The next number in the series is 32. In this series, the numbers increase by *one more with each successive number.* So, there is an increase of 1 between the first two numbers, an increase of 2 between the second and third numbers, an increase of 3 between the third and fourth numbers, and an increase of 4 between the fourth and fifth numbers. The next number in the series should be 5 more than the last number given.

8. D: The correct answer is Matt, Andrew, Geeta. According to the prompt, Andrew watches more television than Geeta. Since the goal is to rank the friends in order of how much television they watch *from most to least,* the list should read the following way so far: Andrew, Geeta. The prompt goes on to say that Andrew watches less television than Matt, so Matt must be added to the list above Andrew.

9. A: The word *notebook* is not like the other three. A pencil, pen, and crayon can all be used to write or draw. A notebook is something that is written or drawn *in,* rendering it different from the other three words.

10. B: The next number in the series is 44. Beginning with the first number in the series, every other number *increases by 1.* Beginning with the second number, every other number *decreases by 1.* So, to find the next number in the series, decide which pattern the missing number should continue. The missing number should continue the pattern of increasing by 1 starting with the first number in the series. Looking only at that pattern, the series reads 41...42...43. Continuing that pattern, the missing number should be 44.

11. D: Out of the three on this particular team, Walt came in first. However, it's unclear whether or not other teams were participating in this race. Thus, there is insufficient information to determine whether or not Walt won the race.

12. B: The next number in the series is 105. In this series, the numbers are decreasing. The gap between each number is either 11 or 3. Following this pattern, the next number should be 11 less than the last number.

13. D: The word *boat* is not like the other three. A lake, ocean, and river are all bodies of water. A boat is a vessel used to traverse bodies of water, rendering it different from the other three words.

14. D: The next number in the series is 9. In this series, each successive number decreases by half.

15. C: Tom's score was 75. According to the prompt, Anna earned 97 points, which was 12 more than Michael. Michael earned 85 points, which is 10 more than Tom.

16. B: The next number in the series is 729. In this series, each number is triple the previous number.

Printed in the USA
CPSIA information can be obtained
at www.ICGtesting.com
LVHW071026181223
766705LV00050B/2832